# NIHILISM AND NEGRITUDE

# NIHILISM AND NEGRITUDE

## WAYS OF LIVING IN AFRICA

*Célestin Monga*

TRANSLATED BY
*Madeleine Velguth*

Harvard University Press

*Cambridge, Massachusetts*
*London, England*
*2016*

Originally published in French as *Nihilisme et négritude: les arts de vivre en Afrique*. Copyright © Presses Universitaires de France, 2009.

*Library of Congress Cataloging-in-Publication Data*
Names: Monga, Célestin, author.
Title: Nihilism and negritude : ways of living in Africa / Célestin Monga ;
translated by Madeleine Velguth.
Other titles: Nihilisme et négritude. English
Description: Cambridge, Massachusetts : Harvard University Press,
2016. | Includes bibliographical references and index.
Identifiers: LCCN 2016006917 | ISBN 9780674970724 (alk. paper)
Subjects: LCSH: Africa, Sub-Saharan—Civilization. | Africa,
Sub-Saharan—Social life and customs. | Blacks—Race
identity. | Nihilism (Philosophy) | Social ethics—Africa,
Sub-Saharan.
Classification: LCC DT14 .M6513 2016 | DDC 967.03/3—dc23
LC record available at http://lccn.loc.gov/2016006917

To the great masters:
*Fabien Eboussi Boulaga, Eugène Ekoumou,*
*Jean-Marc Ela,* and *Ambroise Kom*

For *Maélys* and *Kephren,*
compasses and guardian angels

# CONTENTS

# NIHILISM AND NEGRITUDE

# INTRODUCTION

## NIHILISM: AFRICAN VARIATIONS

So I'm in Douala: no other airport has this picturesque absurdity, this hectic torpor, and this huge dose of bitterness. The customs hall is taken by storm by all manner of individuals whom the damp atmosphere doesn't discourage. As always, you have to wait, interminably, for the luggage. From one and the same flight, bags arrive simultaneously on three carousels—with no explanation. Passengers shove each other rudely, running from one carousel to another as if possessed. In half a century of independence, no one seems to have managed to convince the authorities that the operations of Central Africa's largest airport could be organized differently. In this sort of ambiance, I have to think of Sony Labou Tansi, Emil Cioran, and Fernando Pessoa, and remain calm, free myself of anger, find my suitcase and melt into the waves imposed by this disorder. In this place where officials and embittered citizens alike are convinced they know what they're doing, nothing could be worse than to appear to lecture them.

## A Bantu Back Home

The air laden with sounds and the city's night odors make me quiver. Unjustifiable happiness to be in a geographic space that consciousness has arbitrarily considered as home. Though I travel all over the planet and am received better almost anywhere else, nothing can replace the pleasure that steals beneath my skin the moment I touch Cameroonian soil. Automatic intoxication, enchantment of these places that are part of my memory, untranslatable quivering, indecipherable music of the soul, imperceptible feeling of redemption and eternity.

Yet my happiness is fleeting. Douala no longer has any of its old-fashioned charm felt when contemplating the black and white postcards of a certain era. Pauperization has settled in there with a vengeance, including in the minds of those who claim to administer the city. Walking hurriedly toward some meeting that has suddenly become unimportant, I see spread out everywhere before me a great deal of acrimony. At a turn in the road, I hear anonymous cries escaping from old, dilapidated, wooden houses, those sometimes inhuman cries that no one pays attention to. Cries of pain forgotten in the din of destitution, in the sticky tranquility of the immense collective pain that covers the city.

Bridge across the Wouri: the spectacle is eloquent and symbolic of the worldview that expresses itself in the city. Here, chaos is deconstructed. No traffic signs, no sense of order, no poetry. Drivers seem to be in a trance, all in a hurry. Not a one has enough elegance or generosity to let another go first. Each vehicle moves into the smallest space, without taking into account the supposed direction of traffic flow. Drivers of trucks or powerful cars have an advantage over those driving small automobiles: their steel or simply rusty iron bumpers have sometimes been specially reinforced so they can do the most damage to small vehicles that would have the gall not to give them right of way. Yet everyone behaves like this. Whatever their level of education and their elegance of dress, drivers are equal in their fits of frenzy. Destitution has democratized imbecility. The humid heat and pavement full of potholes stimulate the need for madness. People look daggers at each other. They insult each other copiously while laughing. They cheerfully despise one another. Sometimes with the most obscene gestures and nasty remarks about the other's mother or her body. They threaten to kill each other. They dehumanize one another joyously. Though I grew up in this environment myself, it still takes me a few minutes to readjust my reflexes to it. I notice the optimistic resignation of the good man driving me. He's seen worse.

Automobile traffic in Douala is perhaps the strongest reflection of this civilization that is being engulfed by its own mirages. Several centuries of oppression and fifty years of perverted independence have produced very distinctive ways of thinking and acting and left a good many scars on people's minds. I imagine Cioran finding himself in this shambles. He'd see an infinite number of additional reasons for writing his syllogisms of bitterness. I also imagine a Japanese psychiatrist finding himself in this pandemonium: he'd probably resign from his profession to find another less difficult job, categorically opposed to his presumed competence. Perhaps in plumbing?

Wandering about the city's streets, I hear the noisy silence of the lamentations that are often the fruit of being accustomed to inaction, submitting to the terrorism of discouragement. "So what do we do?" This formula that's heard everywhere, an expression of physical and mental numbness, is paradoxically often punctuated by a disorganized activism that goes so far as to express itself in the explosion of the unofficial economy: it trickles onto the sidewalks, obstructs the streets, and then marginalizes the official economy. It makes me conclude that the first impressions of permanent torpor shouldn't be taken literally. The country's leaders, stultified in their triumphalism, would do well to beware of still waters. Even when they seem to be chloroformed, peoples are capable of eruptions of anger as violent and implacable as tropical storms.

Talking to people of all social classes, I sense the imminence of the revelation: I feel this throbbing and the seismic risk of a political and social tsunami, despite the excitement of the prospect of some sports event or other. The amount of violence governing daily relations—including within families—the volume of prejudice peddled by certain media, the misunderstandings propounded by conversations are so great that one must always remember these words of philosopher Fabien Eboussi Boulaga: "Rwanda is a metaphor or a metonymy for Africa; what happened there is our concern." We must therefore learn to "think the unthinkable."

On the road. From time to time, police officers whom one could mistake for bandits, judged by their getup and the little trust they inspire, stop vehicles according to their mood. Arbitrary prohibitions, great humiliations, little vexations, and a thousand forms of torture make up the daily life of each Cameroonian citizen. To regain my composure and a bit of serenity, I listen to music: Lokua Kanza, whose voice reproduces better than any literature the secrets of this troubled Africa. This music brings me back to Cioran: despite everything, there has to be a paradise, or at least it must have existed—otherwise, where could so much bliss come from?

Kekem, an enigmatic little town, dozing along "National Highway Number 5," which gets narrower as we advance. Despite the beauty of the geography, the place is aggressively dreary. Amazing that everyone there isn't depressed. The inhabitants' good spirits even seem somewhat inappropriate. Suddenly the road disappears under a heap of earth and granite. Already several months ago, a landslide collapsed one of the neighboring hills. The pile of rocks blocked the road. Ten houses were swallowed up. Since then, the administrative authorities and local politicians get together occasionally to . . . discuss possible subjects of discussion. The ministers responsible for these questions have no comment. The "President of the Republic" is too busy playing golf. Is he perhaps contemplating challenging Tiger Woods in the near future?

The state is vacant. Everyone should understand and accept that fact.

A nearby billionaire used part of his personal fortune to have a track cleared around the site of the accident, a detour that now allows vehicles to drive around the obstacle. I ask whether this socially aware action was a subliminal message addressed to the authorities to ironically emphasize their incompetence. I'm told that's not the case. The true reason for his generosity seems to be the imminence of a large funeral ceremony for which he's expecting a great many visitors from all over the world. It would have been annoying if a landslide kept his guests from arriving at his huge mansion, located a few kilometers from there. Cameroonians are fascinated by death—and any bustle that gives the illusion of warding it off. For that matter, at the entrance to the city two huge banners above the road wish a "welcome to the funeral of Papa X . . ." In order to celebrate their cosmogonies and the connection between the living and the dead, poor people go into debt to be able to spend money on funeral ceremonies. I've always thought this strange economy of death had a funereal flavor. But who am I to prescribe happiness to anyone?

Toward midnight. Nocturnal escapade in Bana. The steep road cloaks its mysteries in an immense, immobile mantle of fog. Sweetness and sumptuous majesty of the mountain disappearing into the darkness. The beauty of the moment is so intense that it takes my breath away. Luminous absence of my parents, dazzling memories of my father and mother, buried there, beneath my

feet. They devoted their lives to trying to instill in me the art of measuring a man. I imagine them as circumspect, wondering with doubtful faces about what kind of citizen I've become, about the quality of my existence, about my negritude, about my philosophy of life, about what determines my path, and perhaps about my choice of priorities. I've always missed them greatly. A deep wound with which I travel everywhere, and which will never close.

Traveling toward the south, I stop at Makénéné to buy some watermelon. As always, the vehicle is besieged by women of all ages selling fruit and imploring the travelers to buy some of their organic products, symbols of an agriculture respectful of the environment, farmers, and consumers. These women spend twelve hours a day in the sun or the rain hoping to earn in one week of work barely enough to buy themselves two pounds of meat. There are children here, who I suppose don't go to school, and whose gaze conveys a lack of innocence, a painful indifference. And yet the quality of their products would make consumers of fruit the world over tremble with happiness, particularly in the Arab countries of the Persian Gulf where they're crazy about fresh fruit from Africa. In fifty years, the country's economic strategists have never thought of targeting this huge potential market. A very large quantity of that fruit rotting along the road could, for that matter, be processed on site, create wealth, jobs, added value, and above all contribute its share to the capital of national dignity. Unfortunately, those who govern the country are elsewhere. The "President" is still playing golf. Tiger Woods had better watch out ... As for the

ministers, they're feverishly awaiting the next cabinet re-
shuffle, since there's at least one per year.

Riding through Bafia in the soft sunlight of the afternoon, I have the impression of being plunged into the
night—this great silence that clouds the mind. Certainly,
I can see a few serene men in front of their huts, and silhouettes of women preparing the evening meal. I can also
see children who are laughing. Are they perhaps laughing
at the torpor of the town? Are they perhaps making fun
of the obligatory happiness that I, in my indignation,
would like to prescribe for them?

## Civilized Grief in Yaoundé

The entrance to Yaoundé is a valiant struggle against nothingness: brightly colored, noisy bustle, narrow roadway,
lack of sidewalks, angry horns of taxi drivers and truckers
looking for business, diagonal movements of pedes-
trians, some of whom vaguely look as if they're under the
influence of illegal substances. Behind this disorderly energy, I see the unequal combat of the lower classes against
official contempt and pointlessness.

Downtown. While helping the driver take boxes out of
our vehicle, I scrape the index finger of my right hand.
That's not good just one hour before a book signing session. In the heat of the afternoon, my blood flows with a
vengeance. I rush to the nearest pharmacy for a bandage.
The proprietress treats me with the irritated sharpness
often found in Cameroonian shopkeepers. No, she mutters
with her nastiest air, she doesn't have bandages. I go to

another pharmacy not far from there. Each of the twenty or so customers of all ages pushing toward the counter has only one obsession: to be served first. The latest arrivals have no qualms about pushing and shoving the others to get to the register. No remorse, no guilt. In a suit and tie or a boubou and sandals, rich or poor, speaking French with a Parisian accent or simply mumbling a few words of pidgin English, the customers are satisfied with this random spectacle of humiliation. Grief seems to be flowing through their veins. I ask a member of the pharmacy staff if it wouldn't be better if everyone got in line. He looks at me as if I were a Martian . . .

Later that afternoon. Intense moments at the bookstore where I was signing one of my books. We got started almost on time—a practically exotic little exploit in this city where time has never had the same duration as elsewhere. Braving the humidity and resisting the many pernicious temptations offered by the city at the start of a weekend, Cameroonian intellectuals of all generations had gotten together there, patient, curious, motivated, wanting to engage me in a serious discussion. There were also silently casual onlookers, some of them seeming to be passersby who couldn't afford to buy themselves a book—this object of luxury in the tropics—but wanting to be there, like me, to be part of this precious moment. As a result, the instant was in itself enough: nothing that we might have had to say was of any real importance. This mere ecumenical communion of diverse citizens, engaged in a conversation about themselves, anxious to be the subjects of their history and no longer the objects of the fantasies of others (as the late sociologist Jean-Marc Ela liked to say), was in itself a bit of happiness.

Beyond the ages and supposed political opinions of the group, we began a citizens' dialogue, at times out of step with what I think are the most urgent preoccupations of this people to which we all belong. This meeting beneath the smiling depiction of Mongo Beti, an emblematic figure of dissidence who died in 2001, symbolized rather well the progress made in the past fifteen years or so, despite the stammering of the democratic movement. We were thumbing our noses at a sleepwalking government that thought it had silenced us. So things have come along a bit. The public sphere—this space that, according to Jürgen Habermas, has helped validate the notion of a civil society in the West—has broadened, although stealthily. The obscurantist powers no longer have the means to confiscate all the spaces where speech takes form freely.

Seizing the right to speak is not all, however. Even then, one must use it usefully, and think effectively. Not obvious in a context where intellectual dearth has been maintained for so long that it has managed to seep into the brains of a good many educated people. Today the conversation was polite, the exchanges at times intense. But I really felt the legacy of that despotic grief that imprisons minds. The anger was "civilized" but highly significant. It was expressed against an invisible, immanent evil, against a mysterious, destructive divinity that seemed to have taken control of our history, our present, and our future. It escaped from statements made, slipped into the hot afternoon air, rose into the sky, stirred up minds, animated gestures, made the timbre of voices tremble. An apology of catastrophe, a collective fascination with the ephemeral: I was struck by the calm cynicism of some of my compatriots and their sacrificial need, first and foremost, to find external culprits for the difficulties of Cameroon and Africa. I tried to answer their questions while forcing myself to respect this internal suffering, this despair, this fear of oneself and of the future rushing toward us. I imagined my late father listening to it all with a cryptic grin, lighting a cigarette, and having a beer the better to follow the proceedings. No form of nihilism would have surprised him.

## Pleasure in Nonfulfillment

Stop! Gigantic traffic tie-up about twenty kilometers from Douala. Police officers, made even darker by the terrible rays of the sun, gesticulate furiously in the cacophony of their whistles. Traffic is at a standstill in both directions. No official explanation is given. A driver explains to us that the "Prime Minister" was visiting Douala and was to leave the city at any moment. "For security reasons," all vehicles have been immobilized for a good hour. "You just have to wait . . ."

Walking through this crowd terrorized by its own weakness, I try to understand. In a taxi, passengers are piled onto each other like walking corpses in search of a common grave. Among them, a pregnant woman with a blank stare. I imagine that perhaps she's having second thoughts about the prospect of bringing her child into this kind of world. Around her, the same overwhelmed resignation. The driver uses the collar of his old shirt to fan himself and sighs: "You've got to wonder if God himself hasn't abandoned us." I answer that God is very busy and expects the Cameroonians to take their destiny into their own hands. It does no good to moan inaudibly in the sun's dust.

I ask a friend to find me the phone number of the local police chief. I'm thinking of giving him an ultimatum: if the streets aren't open within the next half hour, I'll try to convince my companions in misfortune and all those undergoing the injustice of being taken hostage in the dusty heat of the place to march on the city. Perhaps there will be only five, ten, or twenty of us; perhaps we'll be shot at by the zealous, sinister-looking soldiers blocking traffic, but by refusing the arbitrariness of official nihilism we'll show this "Prime Minister" and the person behind him that we're now citizens freed of the fear of dying.

I manage to find the number of the head of the criminal investigation department. He doesn't answer. I keep at it. An assistant finally picks up the phone and tells me in sepulchral tones that "the boss is busy." I give her the message that a group of honest citizens, who regularly pay their taxes, is stuck at the entrance to the city on the fallacious pretext that the "Prime Minister" is to come out. I tell her firmly that some of us have decided not to put up with this bad joke any longer, and that we will refuse to comply with police orders if the situation isn't taken care of in the next few minutes. I also let her know that there's a pregnant woman in very bad shape in a taxi parked along the roadway. The assistant in question asks me for my name, my telephone number, and to repeat what I said. Which I do with all the patience I can muster. After listening to me, she asks me if my intention is to "threaten the authorities of the Republic." I make an effort to remain worthy of a reader of Cioran and remind her that, for now, it's the opposite that is going on: the "authorities" are cheerfully torturing good citizens whose only failing was that they were going peacefully about their business. She promises to call me back after talking to her superior. The call in question was not to come.

After an interminable time during which everybody had remained immobilized in the dust, the gloomy motorcade of the "Prime Minister" in question passes at top speed, coming out of the city like a gangster out of a bank building where he's just committed armed robbery. The motorcade goes by quickly in a sinister concert of sirens and horns. I can't help wondering what these people who claim to govern and depend on the army are so afraid of. Unless this is rather a demonstration of their strength? All decadent power has spells to which it clings to give itself confidence, to lie to itself. Seeing my driver's smile, I understand a bit better the disenchanted serenity of my many compatriots. Faced with the absurd, several attitudes are possible. One would consist of organizing an active revolt, of lapsing into an agitated frenzy that would quickly verge on frivolity. In countries where political regimes have often manifested their cannibalism, this approach would not only be ineffective: it would, philosophically, be rather simplistic and naïve. Another approach to the situation would consist of opposing imbecility with a subtle scorn, snickering at it. My driver favors this "lucid stupidity" that Enrique Vila-Matas sometimes speaks of: in a time of generalized mindlessness, the wise person should pretend to be an idiot. The character of Erasmus's fool *(In Praise of Folly),* for that matter, said the same thing: in this great theater that is human existence, each person should continue to play his part, without being taken in, knowing how to assume the comic consciousness that is appropriate to certain situations. Faced with power's arbitrariness, silence is not necessarily complicity. It is sometimes elegance of the soul and pedagogy of indifference. I certainly wasn't expecting such a lesson in nihilism from my driver!

Later that evening. A mischievous friend takes me to the famous nightclub Le Privé. He explains that, to correctly penetrate the secrets of a city like Douala, you have to take its nocturnal temperature. I go with the soul of an ethnologist. The music's racket is anchored to a heavy, monotonous beat. It may be joyous, but it sounds like a death wish around which boisterous dancers express their thirst for life. In this collective desire to reduce what can only be a very serious deficiency of frenzy, women are the most frenzied. At times their movements express something like a need to lose consciousness, a renunciation of the here and now. Looking at them, I disregard the music and wonder about the possible reasons for these

trances, this trembling, this determination that they each
have to leave their bodies, perhaps to drown themselves
in the illusory foam of the night. What would Pessoa
have thought of such a nihilism of sensual pleasure?

"They don't know that heaven and hell are the efflo-
rescences of a second, of a single second" (Cioran). The
sparkle of an instant satisfies. I make out in certain
blank, absent looks a habituation to grief, the scars and
torments of daily life, and the fear of seeing prospects
fray too quickly. Not having the luxury of being able to
think of the future, these people are afraid of time and
hurl themselves body and soul into the slightest chances
offered by the present moment. They desperately flee
their past and believe they'll find crumbs of happiness
in the vapors of alcohol. Smoking also helps them con-
ceal their emotions. Some ostensibly brandish fat cigars—
Montecristo No. 2—that help them have confidence in
themselves. They seem to delight in their lack of accom-
plishment. Done up tight in a tired suit, one of my immediate neighbors feverishly serves champagne to his partner
and kisses her distractedly from time to time, which
doesn't prevent him from threatening what he'll do if
she misbehaves. Observing him, I think of the emperor
Caligula who never kissed his wife's or mistresses' necks
without reminding them that it was within his power to
have their throats slit.

My stay in Cameroon ends in a rush, in the obvious frustration of not having had time for myself or for others—and
above all not having been able to pick up other manifestations of this philosophy of existence that is perhaps the

latest incarnation of negritude. When I'm back in Washington, a friend asks me about the meaning of all these images that have remained in my memory. What to think of this my country that has been living below its means for so long and is, in many respects a metaphor not only of sub-Saharan Africa, but also of what is generally called the black world? How to help reduce the deficits of vision, self-esteem, self-confidence, and leadership that benumb minds and dilute dreams of happiness? While we talk, I look out the window. The bushes are immobile in the immaculate greenness of a mild winter. Clean and sanitized. As for my American neighbors, they don't ask metaphysical questions. They get up every morning and do whatever their duty prescribes for them. Exactly, for that matter, like Mami Madé, my grandmother still living in her village. But she lives in a universe where mores are for the moment quite different from America's dominant values.

It is therefore important to try to understand my compatriots' objective choices and their desire for offhandedness. To understand the ineffectiveness of ethical fervor in Africa. To explain the propensity for cynicism in individual and collective action, the essence of daily life in various spheres of the black world. To ponder the philosophical hypotheses underlying the discrepancy in paths between our universe and the world.

## Beyond the Bad and the Worst

The vignettes and slices of life arbitrarily compiled above, as I happened to run across them during my peregrinations in Cameroon, illustrate something quite different from material poverty. Anecdotal though they may be, they reflect other aspects of the existential misery that characterizes the social transformations taking place in Africa. The intellectual debate on often observed behaviors, their causes and consequences, tends to overlook the complexity of the phenomena observed, and especially the philosophical questions that underlie them. It is too often reduced to a dialogue of the deaf between representatives of diverse ideological coteries.

What is it that we hear? Roughly speaking, there are two opposing types of discourse on Africa and, more generally, the black world.[1] On one hand, there is a certain structuralism that explains the chaos and pauperization on the continent by historic, political, and economic factors (slavery, colonization, exploitation, dependence, dictatorships, and bad governance). The theoreticians of structuralism stress the weight of the injustices and historical arbitrariness in the destructuration and the *commodification* of African societies, as well as the construction of an international order intended to instrumentalize them, to marginalize them in the world economy. This literature, tinged with whining and bitterness, is often produced by left-wing intellectuals.

The second vision of Africa is that of the culturalists, for whom the continent's griefs are above all due to personal choices, to individual or collective decisions, and to behaviors. Considering that the black world does not have a monopoly on suffering and injustice, they point out that other communities have been able to overcome history's curses and come out of oppression. They claim that Africans, on the contrary, locked themselves either into a primitive nationalism or a sterile anger concerning the past, posing in the eyes of the world as eternal victims who have nothing to offer the conscience of humanity but their lamentations and their venom. They would thus be, in a way, among those peoples who exploit misfortune to the point of trivializing tragedy (Cioran). Their habituation to what is bad and their passive acceptance of the worst would thus simply be the logical consequence of a philosophical attitude that rejects the notion of personal responsibility.

A simplistic dichotomy thus opposes, on one hand, the sometimes saccharine humanism of the "structuralists" (progressives), who tend to infantilize the African peoples by finding external justifications for all the continent's ills and, on the other hand, the scorn of the "culturalists" (conservatives), who perceive them as communities permeated by a taste for sadomasochism and cynicism. This confrontation serves up views of the continent that are nothing but caricatures. First because it is illusory to attempt to distinguish the external causes of the moral and political crisis from which the black world has been suffering for almost four centuries from the internal ones. The orders of values and the social norms that determine the ethical architecture, behaviors, and culture of a place are indissolubly linked to the prevailing political and economic dynamics. Next, the distinction between structural and cultural factors is also arbitrary. The institutions that issue and sanction rules and conducts (families, schools, religious organizations, etc.) are themselves constantly influenced by the political and economic structures in force, and vice versa.

More important: this debate focuses on the usual clichés concerning the black world and amplifies their impact. Structuralists and culturalists too often dwell on the symptoms of the crisis and not on its causes. Both sides repeatedly tick off, either to deplore them or endorse them, the habituation to poverty, the superficial and sensualist elites' focus on the sordid side of life, the hedonism of the lower classes, the perpetual need for entertainment, the passive acceptance of a meaningless existence, the chronic anger and silent social rage that seem to be part and parcel of the social fabric, the repeated spasms of violence that mark the political landscape, the permanent despair, the taste for sadomasochism, and the unacknowledged temptation to collective suicide . . . This evades the underlying philosophical question—that is, the deeper justification of the attitudes and mores often observed across the entire black world.

Now, to understand certain social and political dynamics that are manifested in daily life in sub-Saharan Africa and within the diaspora, it is necessary to go beyond the generally listed and condescendingly expressed pathologies. The paternalistic and superficial reading of the difficulties of Africa and Africans must be abandoned, and the philosophical substratum and patterns of reasoning concealed behind the most ordinary behaviors of daily life must be seriously explored. This must be done without giving in to the misused generalizations that tend to be inferred based on anecdotal evidence. This is

the major error committed by the initiators of the movement called Negritude that, beginning in the late 1920s,
strove to celebrate Negro-African values.

## Negritude, Conformism, and Dissidence

"Negritude" is one of those terms that are blunted by
their own history. It is therefore advisable to attempt to
define it clearly before using it. Appearing for the first
time in 1935 in an article by Aimé Césaire in the journal
*L'Étudiant noir,* it designated above all a literary and political movement. It attempted to express "the totality of
the cultural values of the black world" (Léopold Sédar
Senghor), and to use these as a basis for the revaloriza-
tion of the contested humanity of the Negro-African
peoples. It thus defined both an attitude of philosophical pride and the intellectual scaffolding of a political
movement of recognition of an oppressed people, which
was, at the time, still under colonial dominance. It is
moreover impossible to evaluate the impact of Negritude without resituating it in the context of its historic
beginnings.

Its proponents, moreover, considered their action as
following an old, black, American tradition of dissidence
and valorization of an identity scorned by the slave trade
and slavery.[2] The word "negritude," standard of this revolt, took up in French the idea of blackness, already in
vogue in the writings of American authors like Langston
Hughes, Richard Wright, and others active in the Harlem

Renaissance.[3] Negritude was therefore at its origin a medium of reappropriation of the dignity of oppressed peoples. In his 1948 preface to Senghor's *Anthologie de la poésie nègre*, Jean-Paul Sartre was feverishly enthusiastic about this speaking out by people who had so long been confined to silence, stating with charming naïveté: "Negro poetry is angelic, it comes bearing glad tidings; negritude is found again."[4] This angelism could not remain innocent for long. By positioning itself as a counterattack to white domination, Negritude was based on the idyllic and luxurious vision of a black world that, in reality, had never existed. It is true that Negritude as a simple refusal of suffering and exaltation of the joy of dancing and of laying claim to a "black personality" enabled the new African political leaders and elites to give themselves a place in the sun. But precisely because it focused on the question of race, it neglected, for instance, class problems.

In the late 1960s, Césaire, from the French West Indies, had tried to re-place Negritude into its historical context, insisting on its role as a link between groups of populations sharing a common history filled with suffering and humiliation: "It's a movement affirming the solidarity of the blacks of the Diaspora with the African world. You know, one isn't black with impunity, and whether one is French—of French culture—or whether one is of American culture, there is one essential fact: namely, that one is black, and that that matters. That's Negritude. It affirms a solidarity. On one hand, in time, with our black ancestors and this continent from which we've come (three centuries ago, that's not that long), and then a horizontal solidarity between all the people who came from there and who have this heritage in common. And we feel that this heritage matters; it still weighs on us; so we should not renounce it but make it bear fruit—in different ways no doubt—according to the current state of affairs—and in view of which we are obliged to react" (interview in the *Magazine littéraire,* 1969). So Negritude as epigraph of a particular experience of life common to peoples disseminated across Africa, the Caribbean, America, and Europe. Negritude as the updating of a human heritage that several centuries of bloody history have not completely erased. Negritude as a philosophical *aggiornamento* necessary to the restoration of an imaginary wounded by the injustices of oppression, but still capable of reinventing itself to face the necessities and urgencies of the moment.

And yet, these remarks have not prevented many African intellectuals from criticizing the racial foundations of Negritude, and from scoffing at its ineffectiveness and uselessness. "A tiger does not proclaim his tigritude, he pounces," stated the Nigerian Wole Soyinka . . . The fact that Senghor, after being president of Senegal, retired to Normandy and finished his philosophic journey in the French Academy enabled critics of Negritude to conclude that this movement was in reality a posturing by African intellectuals with hang-ups, seeking their own validation in the eyes of others. Negritude then would only have been a conformist attitude, a pseudo-dissidence where people dream of coming close to a mysterious norm of humanity defined by the former colonizers.

"I belong to broad daylight," proclaims the Cameroonian poet Paul Dakeyo, one of the most acerbic critics of Senghor's Negritude. As for me, I belong to the generation of Africans born just after the wave of independence and I don't feel I have anything to do with these Byzantine identity quarrels organized around the black race. Beyond the essentialism of racial theories and the illusion of solidarity linked to supposed skin color, there is above all the tireless erosion of time. What is there actually between the philosophy of life of an African American billionaire from Chicago like Oprah Winfrey and that of the Senegalese women selling trinkets on the streets of New York or Dakar? What commonality is there between a Barack Obama—born of a Kenyan father who practically didn't know him and an American mother from Kansas who raised him in Hawaii and Indonesia—and his brothers and cousins in Nairobi whose existence he wasn't even aware of and with whom he's never had a relationship? What is the significance of biology in a world where black and white now come in an infinite palette of colors? The myth of the racial homogeneity of the black world and of the worldviews that are supposed to ensue from it does not stand up to analysis.

Today's Africans are often citizens of the world, even when they haven't left the land of their birth. Technological progress and the developments of communication now allow Mali farmers to know in real time the decisions and actions of Zimbabwean or Indian cotton planters. In the same way, Cameroonian students can, via the Internet, take all the economics courses taught by the professors of the Massachusetts Institute of Technology in Boston. Human rights activists in Ghana can virtually follow live on television the development of the political situation in Darfur or Ethiopia. The world is much more accessible than half a century ago. The consequence: our imaginaries draw, much more than is thought, from the philosophic heritage of that world, to which we all belong. Negritude as a philosophy of life could not be today what it was yesterday. That is why historian Achille Mbembe speaks of an "Afropolitanism" that would designate the emergence of a new cultural, historic, and aesthetic sensibility, of the "awareness of the interweaving of the here and there, the presence of the elsewhere in the here and vice versa, the relativization of primary roots and memberships and the way of embracing, with full knowledge of the facts, strangeness, foreignness and remoteness, the ability to recognize one's face in that of a foreigner and make the most of the traces of remoteness in closeness, to domesticate the unfamiliar, to work with what seem to be opposites."[5]

Like millions of other Africans, I strongly feel that I am an heir to this long tradition of exchanges that invalidates all biological and racial fetishism. Civilizations are not impermeable chemical particles. That said, some manage the process of fusion-absorption better than others. No one would say, for example, that China is no longer "Chinese" because, in five thousand years of history it has integrated customs of Asia Minor or Japan. The interweaving of the here and there in each of us is an undeniable fact, but it does not operate with the same intensity everywhere and its results are not uniform. The phenomenon that consists of melting oneself into cultures that have come from elsewhere does not affect everyone, and certainly not to the same degree. And then, if all the world's citizens had the same cultural baggage, we would very quickly end up being identical. There would no longer be any need for a mixing of cultures. I therefore certainly define myself as a citizen of the world, but African in spite of everything. It is from the viewpoint of this syncretic "Africanness" (or, put differently, this new negritude) that I act, observe my fellow humans, and interpret their thoughts.

## The Phantomatic African: The Question of Otherness

So, African. But who am I precisely? An African of the great diaspora or of the continent? Who are we? How do we know what we are? What indisputable criteria define us today? How much arbitrariness is acceptable in this categorization imposed by others or by ourselves? How shall we think through the question of otherness in this global village where Africa is, incidentally, only an invention?—this is what philosophers Kwame Anthony

Appiah of Ghana and Valentin Y. Mudimbe of the Congo discuss masterfully.[6] These questions should be approached with moderation, avoiding both the snares of identitary rationalism and the superficial universalism of those who believe that citizens of Douala, Bamako, Copenhagen, or Tokyo have the same history and give the same meanings to their behaviors.

"All of us, at some moment, have had a vision of our existence as something unique, untransferable and very precious. This revelation almost always takes place during adolescence. Self-discovery is above all the realization that we are alone: it is the opening of an impalpable, transparent wall—that of our consciousness—between the world and ourselves."[7] These words of Octavio Paz mark out the framework of all meditation about oneself and others. A common life experience is important. But it could never erase completely the labyrinth of solitude, which is the lowest common denominator of human experience. That is why the original Negritude, like all hasty and in some ways totally artificial categorizations, has been sharply criticized. Its nativist postulate of solidarity linked to skin color, its racial constructs, and its exploitation for political ends by unscrupulous political entrepreneurs amply justify indignation.

All the same. To speak reasonably about Africa and the black world today is to go beyond polemics and the froth of words to explore the criteria of this subjectivity that sometimes asserts itself noisily in ways of thinking, (provisional) philosophies of life, norms, mores, and social practices. This artificial but patiently constructed otherness, asserted and acknowledged, is particularly pronounced among many Africans, especially in these times when the acceleration of globalization is forcing the continent to reassess itself.

We must bring ourselves to face the squaring of the circle with which we are confronted and understand, like Antonio Machado, that "the other does not exist," because it is ourselves. Or that the image of oneself, of that stranger we see every morning in the bathroom mirror, is perhaps much more undecipherable and more distant than that of the neighbor across the hall or the people we rub shoulders with every day on the street. In real life, this other who we think is fictional never lets itself be intimidated or eliminated. Like those characters in science fiction movies whom the hero thinks he's gotten rid of in every duel, it quickly reassembles the pieces of its mysterious body and always returns in force, often at the moment when we least expect it. It "subsists and persists; it is the hard bone on which reason breaks its teeth." Must we then accept "the essential Heterogeneity of being," or "the incurable otherness from which oneness must always suffer"?[8] Perhaps it would be wise to make the best of it and try to understand the acute consciousness that we each have of our singularity. But it is advisable to remember Octavio Paz's warning: "We could distinguish ourselves from other peoples by our creations rather than by the dubious originality of our character, which was the result, perhaps, of constantly changing circumstances."[9] That, by the way, seems to me to be the condition of an ethics of difference.

The object of this essay is not to offer an African philosophy of existence, but to propose ways of seeing and
acting within restricted groups that, rightly or wrongly,
assert the consciousness of being Africans or belonging
to a black world. I realize the risks and pitfalls of such an
endeavor. But it seems possible to me to talk about the
African continent while avoiding the failings and conceptual dead ends both of the nativism of those who imagine
it as a homogenous, bioracial whole, and of the "African
cultural authenticity" in which those who are nostalgic for
a paradise lost continue to revel. Here, African American
sociologist Orlando Patterson's distinction between "thick"
identity and "thin" identity seems useful: thick identity
would designate the philosophical foundation of the
promotion of an autonomous, "African-style" reasoning,
unique, separatist, and exclusive, meant to legitimize a
nefarious rationality of difference. This is obviously not
the goal of this study. Thin identity, deliberately more in-
distinct in its contours, would refer to a shared vision of
collective interests, a certain indefinable inclusivity enabling Africans of all kinds to learn from the wounds and
scars of their common history in order to imagine and
construct an open future.

Readers who are lazy or in a hurry should then not
seek in this little work the brooding figure of an African
citizen defined exclusively, nor the traces of a mysterious
rationality specific to Africa, nor even the philosophical
marks of the hazy and unstable notion of collective identity. The group solidarities that underlie the nihilistic

views analyzed here are neither exclusive nor immutable. In an increasingly interactionistic world, they have nothing to do with biology or race. African nihilisms are moreover incompatible with the existence of a single, immobile, immanent African rationality. They rather stress the need to take in a diversity of dynamic approaches striving toward reason. "Bottom-up" rationalities (those of the populations) should be the focus of analysis and essential postulates to those who would like to accede to the infinite philosophical truths of Africa—a region of the world that has long been neglected in the name of an alleged "top-down" knowledge (that of the elites), and a people kept outside its own history.

It would of course be naïve to deny the heritage of Negritude and nationalism in mentalities, and the fact that some citizens of Africa or Africans of the diaspora continue to dream of the existence of an African culture, if not impermeable, then at least specific, destined to serve as a foundation to individual and collective identities. I do not refute the illusion of distinct forms of African cultural productions reflecting ways of seeing the world and reasoning in certain situations. But my goal is to analyze the modes of psychological management of this intellectual legacy, and to show that the African peoples take the liberty of conforming to them, differentiating themselves from them, or even reinventing them through various forms of nihilism.

## Cioran and Schopenhauer in the Tropics

Schopenhauer was probably not acquainted with the African American ghettos of Los Angeles. Nietzsche probably had a very small readership in Zambia. Cioran wasn't familiar with the pagan music of Salvador de Bahia, and he had never visited Brazil, Mali, or Cameroon. Thomas Bernhard did not develop his reflections on the imperative of suicide while strolling down the streets of Addis Ababa or Kinshasa. And yet, the different variants of their nihilist philosophies are practiced there daily by men and women wishing, like me, to live their negritude differently. The object of this little work is to present several aspects of this approach to existence that is now very popular in the whole of the black world.

Nihilism is one of those philosophical concepts that mean so many different things that they finally arouse confusion more than anything else. Let us therefore try to clarify the thesis of this work a bit by going over some of the conceptions of nihilism. The first is connected to the etymology of the word itself (*nihil,* "nothing" in Latin) and refers to what Paul Bourget called a "terminal life fatigue, a doleful perception of the vanity of all effort."[10] The often tragic history of the past four centuries offers Africans of the continent and the diaspora sufficient material to sustain their anger. This terminal life fatigue was moreover the money-maker of the various revolutionary movements, from Marcus Garvey's "Negro-African fundamentalism" to the radical theories of violence of the Black Panthers. It was also the ferment of the "pragmatic nationalism" of Martin R. Delany, a militant black nineteenth-century American abolitionist and founder of black nationalism and also of Negritude, defined as a positive and transforming explosion of anger.

Another approach to nihilism consists in celebrating the absurd and nothingness, to the point of scorning not only any attempt to change society, but also the justification of any action at all. This is Nietzsche's metaphysics, that of the death of God and the obsolescence of the values orienting human action, that of pessimism and vacuity, which nonetheless makes us capable of "loving life without there being a reason for it" (Raphaël Enthoven). A great many Africans of all social strata don't need to steep themselves in Cioran's aphorisms to cultivate skepticism, as well as an inconsolable melancholy. That does not prevent them from surviving anxiety and from rejecting suicide—this illusion of a better world after death.

A third reading of nihilism, derived from the preceding one, is the necessity to set oneself a goal in life, despite its obvious uselessness, and to develop a philosophy of existence even when one knows that everything has the same beginning and the same end, and that we are all going cheerfully toward our deaths. On this basis, many of my Cameroonian compatriots and millions of other African citizens across the planet feel contempt for all transcendence. Dismissing both the gods and the devils produced by human imaginaries and managed by the theological institutions that dominate the faith market, they celebrate the meaninglessness of existence and participate with remarkable talent and creativity in the construction of this "active nihilism" spoken of by Gianni Vattimo and others.

These different variations of nihilism make it possible to interpret the images I observe in my country and to harmonize them with philosophical paradigms prevailing there. They perhaps also lead to a better understanding of the ordinariness of this Africa and this black world that some insist, in the name of an irreducible otherness, on keeping out of the "mainstream" of world thought. But the fact of placing certain behaviors into an appropriate perspective and identifying the various forms of nihilism that can be associated with the modes of thinking and today's negritude would be only a stage in the philosophical reflection on the black world. Why? Because "this morning I *thought* for a whole hour, that is I deepened my uncertainties a bit more," says Cioran.[11]

A word, finally, on the methodological liberties I take in this book. Negritude as today's African condition, often caricatured by the media and reduced to a sad symphony of suffering, is a subject of great philosophical intensity. Of course the ordinary citizens of Douala or Bamako do not discuss metaphysics or epistemology directly. Yet many of them question their actions daily and try to situate their decisions and acts under the aegis of a moral philosophy—and thus of a code of ethics—that is worthwhile. It would be appropriate to seize this unquenchable thirst for morality that governs behaviors which one would a priori consider the most "immoral" in order to "open the eyes of the naïve" and extract the truth they sometimes keep buried under their lies. So it is, in a way, a matter of using microphilosophy to decipher the absurd. The means of access is thus indirect: not by the presentation of a general theory and system of reasoning, but by details and sequences, in an often allusive manner.

The choice made here is that of meditating on themes chosen as they happen to come up in my dreams and musings, rather than developing a mechanically constructed system of thought. Empiric observation is sometimes completed by commentaries on certain texts by African and African American authors, without aiming at exegetical discussions. I have in mind Michel Foucault's critique of the working methods of established philosophers: "The reduction of discursive practices to textual traces; the elision of the events produced therein and the retention only of marks for a reading; the invention of voices behind texts to avoid having to analyze the modes of implication of the subject in discourses; the assigning of the originary as said and unsaid in the text to avoid placing discursive practices in the field of transformations where they are carried out."[12] My working method in this book will rather be comparable to what musicians call the modes of "synchronization": instead of developing a thesis by going from the general theme to specific observations, I shall proceed by forms of parallelism, stressing the relationship between general principles and particular facts, the anecdote, reflection, and theme at times merging, with the aim of mutually reinforcing each other. My approach, which refutes all generalization, actually comes down to imagining what certain ways of thinking and living bring to philosophy. Or how Cioran, Schopenhauer, and the others would perhaps have modified and enriched their nihilisms if they had had the equivocal good fortune to live in today's tropics.

# 1

## DESIRE'S RUSES

### POLITICAL ECONOMY OF MARRIAGE

Love: is it to love or to be loved?
—J. B. MPIANA, Congolese artist

There is no such thing as love. There are only evidences of love.
—JEAN COCTEAU, screenplay for *Les dames du bois de Boulogne*

The chauffeur had taken me to the Koulouba fruit market in Ouagadougou (Burkina Faso) where I wanted to get a supply of organic oranges and strawberries. Those they served at the four-star hotel where I was staying seemed hopelessly lacking in juice and flavor. They gave the impression of having been imported, frozen, and dried in dust to punish the potbellied expatriate guests permanently tanning next to the pool. I was in Burkina Faso on one of those official World Bank trips that mobilize all the members of a country's government and senior civil service for two weeks. As head of mission I had at my disposal a chauffeur and an impressive black, government Mercedes. It was quite practical for getting around quickly in the city's traffic jams, but not very discrete for going shopping in an ordinary market. So I'd hesitated before asking the chauffeur to take me to the market in such a showy vehicle. But, besides the fact that I didn't have much time for this little trip, I needed a translator to capture the mood of this place of trade where Mooré, one of the national languages, was the only true medium of communication.

The first seller who had threaded her way through the stalls to bring me her tray of fruit had "earned her day" as they say there: I'd bought all her merchandise for double her asking price. She'd given me a stunned look, wiping her black forehead dripping with sweat—Ouagadougou in February is as mild as a boiling volcano. In her deliciously broken French, she'd asked me whether I wanted anything else for the rest of the money. I had the chauffeur explain to her in Mooré that I didn't want anything else, that this extra amount was a tip and that I admired her courage—you really need courage to spend your days in the harsh, burning sun waiting for hypothetical buyers of oranges. She was an adolescent of about sixteen whose smile was both timid and intimidating. I'd asked her if she went to school. She'd lowered her glance to explain that she'd had to give up her studies and that all she did in life was sell fruit to help her mother.

At that moment, an old lady who was watching our exchange, seated on a box not far from there, had gotten up and approached with difficulty. Her eyes held a look of empty sadness, a nothingness contemplating itself. She'd made a furtive grimace that I'd interpreted as a smile and said a few words that the chauffeur had translated hesitantly, with an amused expression:

"She's the girl's mother. She's suggesting you take her daughter with you."

"Take the girl with me? But where and what for?"

"For whatever you want," the chauffeur had explained, translating the old lady's instructions. "She could work for you as a cook or even become your wife."

Momentarily speechless with surprise, I'd made sure that I'd understood this impromptu dialogue correctly. The old lady's toothless smile had become more insistent and the intense look in her eyes had made me realize she was seriously expecting an answer.

"I'm only a stranger passing through . . ."

"That doesn't matter."

"Tell her that maybe I'm happily married . . ."

"In that case, she'll be your second wife!" the old woman had replied, unperturbed and apparently insisting that the driver translate her words faithfully.

The girl was following the exchange with an inscrutable expression. I wondered whether the kindness with which she looked at me reflected chiefly fear of her mother.

"What does the girl think of her mother's suggestion?" I'd asked the chauffeur, convinced that then I'd have a forceful argument against this indecent proposal.

This question had inserted a bit of gravity into the conversation, and the translator had, for once, taken on a serious air to put my question to the old woman.

Unflustered, she'd retorted that she knew her daughter well enough to affirm that she shared her opinion. To show that she didn't want to intimidate the young girl, she suggested leaving us alone a few moments so the two of us could discuss the matter. "You'll see for yourself that my daughter would be happy to leave with you," she'd concluded as she walked away.

"Not so fast!" I insisted. "That's not necessary. Your daughter doesn't know me—or you either for that matter. A marriage can't be arranged in a few seconds at a market. Maybe I'm a lowlife . . ."

"I don't think so."

". . . or a drug dealer . . ."

"My daughter is a good girl, well brought-up; she cooks perfectly and knows how to do everything very well. There's no way you'll regret this . . . And then, if after trying her out you don't want her, you can always bring her back to me. No problem . . ."

No problem?

The girl was still silent, smiling, timid. I'd looked around to try to assess what the other fruit sellers thought of this conversation. Impossible to decipher their serene, detached air.

Why me?

Had she simply been impressed by the huge official vehicle and the chauffeur's barely concealed obsequiousness, signs of my power and importance? Was it the money—the fact that I'd offered far more than the price of the fruit? Did this old procuress spend her days at the market of-

fering her daughter to all the customers who arrived at her stall in a big car?

"I looked at you; I believe in my instincts and my heart. I'm certain you're a decent guy. My daughter would be happy with you. I'm sure my daughter loves you."

An explanation that may have satisfied my ego, but didn't help me understand.

"My daughter suffers too much here at the market, and seeing her suffer makes me suffer."

So that was it! It was simply a matter of trying to free the pretty adolescent from destitution, of finding employment for her. I had in the end kindly refused the offer and left, followed by the tearful gazes of mother and daughter. Not, by the way, without thinking of Keats: "I am a coward. I cannot bear the pain of being happy."[1]

Yet, on the days that followed I kept thinking of that conversation, rather uncommon in this area of the Sahel where, despite material poverty, mores and customs celebrate pride and dignity.[2] The love of which I had suddenly been the target at this dusty market had run straight into my skepticism. Had I missed something? Didn't biologists claim that one falls in love if, and only if, one secretes pheromones emitted by little glands located beneath one's nose and sent like a message to influence the behavior of the other? What were the respective parts of chance and calculation in this business? Would my supposed charm have operated as effectively in other circumstances? Would those women have "loved" me as suddenly if I'd arrived, not in a big, black Mercedes but on foot, and if I'd

nervously bargained down the price of the oranges like most of the other customers, instead of offering to pay twice what I'd been asked? What had become of the art of seduction?

This impromptu exchange led me to attempt to reflect on the determinants of love in new African couples. Perhaps, in their theory of affects, this girl and her intrepid mother saw love simply as the immanent desire for another supposedly matching my profile. After all, doesn't Jorge Luis Borges tell us that "to love is to feel that we are missing something"?[3] Perhaps to them love was above all a desire for transcendence, the wish to cling to a man deemed capable of getting them out of a difficult social condition. Love would then be, before anything else, an ideality anchored in concern for oneself. Or perhaps they defined it as the true love of Marsilio Ficino, that is a desire for beauty: not the ephemeral beauty of the body that arouses the primitive senses (touch, smell, taste), but the eternal beauty that appeals to the senses called "noble" (sight, hearing, reason). Perhaps, finally, they had that nihilistic conception of the sentiments that I had at times observed in various social milieus in Africa, which consists in removing from love its affective and moral dimension to give it above all a utilitarian significance.

### Nihilistic Love

Sociologists are categorical: African women's motivations for marriage have changed a great deal in one gen-

eration. The feeling of being in love, which was long put forward, along with the necessity to conform to cultural practices and family demands, has given way to more materialistic considerations. The lack of self-confidence that formerly compelled them to resort to the most eccentric seduction techniques to find a husband and be accepted socially seems to be disappearing totally. The liberation of female desires is now comparable to what took place in the West in the 1960s with the advent of feminism. The only major difference: here it is not accompanied by indignant denunciations of "woman as object." And for good reason: if the woman is desired for her beauty, the African "man as object" is also sought after for his purchasing power and social status.

Freed of guilt, African women fight their affective deficit by inventing for themselves a new justification of conjugal love. They marry less and less frequently out of respect for social conventions or for sentimental reasons, but rather to give depth to their existence and move into psychological territory to which they would not have access on their own. Wishful thinking makes no one happy and conjugal happiness defined as being in love is moreover not a viable goal of existence. Like Georg Christoph Lichtenberg, they believe that if love is blind, marriage will restore its sight. Better to remain lucid and not cede to this "smoke raised with the fume of sighs" (Shakespeare, *Romeo and Juliet,* act I, scene 1).

The way they view their flirtation with a stranger nicely symbolizes this new nihilism of love. The sometimes furtive and casual aspect of the first romantic encounter

also reveals a certain conception of the family they intend to create: one that rejects the illusion of the osmotic
couple where men and women are guided by their feelings alone. The couple is seen as a thing too important to
be abandoned to the chance of emotions. The so-called
traditional model of African marriage described with
naïve enthusiasm by anthropologist and ethnologist
Claude Lévi-Strauss, uniting not two individuals but several entire families, still exists. But young people make
no secret of new motivations: they marry less often to
perpetuate tradition and honor their ancestors than to
position themselves on the social ladder and obtain the
supplementary purchasing power indispensable to as-
suming their status.

Thus, whether he is unexpectedly approached at a fruit
market, on the street or in a nightclub, or whether he
is found by a relative playing the role of intrepid go-
between, the potential husband is instinctively weighed
and evaluated by his future ladylove: his ability to effectively take on the social role of the ideal partner is deliberately sized up. Love[4] is no longer reduced to an alchemy
of sensations felt at chance encounters; it is seen as a nihilistic enterprise celebrating the difference between the
sexes and the cult of male-female alterity. Value is thus
given to the minute but incompressible distance existing
between the sexes. Men are urged to follow the sort of ad-
vice formulated by Jorge Luis Borges, that is, to feel and
savor "that so pleasant something there is in a woman, in
any woman; that something which, of course, cannot be
defined but which quite simply makes it enjoyable to be

with a woman. This has nothing to do with love or sensuality; it's the fact, let's say, of this slight difference, a difference that is very slight but sufficient to be perceived and, at the same time, close enough that it does not separate us."[5]

In such a context, the narcissistic questions that generally underlie a romantic encounter ("What does he think of me?"; "Does he think I'm pretty?") are replaced by more concrete preoccupations: "What's the social standing of this possible future partner?"; "What can he offer me?"; "Is he able to free my family of financial worries?" And as the future lovers or husbands are asking themselves these same questions, the romantic relationship is stripped of the naïve optimism that threatens it. Paradoxically, this egalitarian beginning of the relationship is actually the source of a new idealism that is more solid, for it is based not on the secret dream of some abstract happiness, but rather on the reality of mutual needs to satisfy.

So no more wandering about in a useless labor of seduction manifested in other societies by a courtship as romantic as it is extreme. Here, love at first sight, the instant discovery of affinities that Roland Barthes called "reciprocal proliferation," is above all the unadorned recognition, by two individuals, of their common emotional or conjugal interests. Voltaire claimed that the steps of seduction are rather simplistic, men being interested in the visual and women in what they are told. "You catch a woman by her ears and a man by his eyes," he stated. The author of *The Maid of Orleans* would have been a very poor seducer in Ouagadougou, where the mechanisms of mutual attraction used by individuals of the two sexes are focused above all on the cost-benefit analysis of a possible relationship. Because not much can be expected of sentiments, emotions are rationalized. Increasingly frequent recourse to online meeting sites facilitates the work of selection, which is not only a time saver but also helps identify the ideal partner more precisely.

Romanticizing the myth of love as is often done in couples' relationships in the West is thus less and less popular in Africa. Instead, the fundamental principle to be conformed to recommends limiting the blunders of the imaginary that are the consequence of an excessive faith in the mythical virtues of love and excessive expectations concerning conjugal life. Of course, as everywhere else, crimes of passion and suicides due to disappointed love do exist. But here they are met with disapproval, scorn, and the condemnation of those guilty of them. Being unhealthily "in love" with one's partner to the point of killing oneself or committing a crime in the name of this feeling is seen by many Africans as the boast of a weakling, the luxury of idle, bourgeois, or *Westernized* individuals. For love is an aestheticized illusion, "a construct, a social invention and not a 'natural' phenomenon. In that, it scarcely differs from many things that surround us and that we take for granted, whereas they are the result of a long historical movement of formation, of the working out of a particular meaning."[6] Love is the "happiness of a madman," a completely abnormal feeling, since it is accompanied by all the troubled states that ordinarily characterize a deranged mind: anxiety, morbid suspicion, despair, paranoia, egoism, devilish ferocity, and so forth.

Love is therefore demystified by taking away its venom. To that end, one avoids letting oneself be overwhelmed by feelings. The exaltation of marriage and the arbitrary attachment to a being who is not oneself bear the seeds of an emotional catastrophe. In an absolute perspective, the emotional benefits of the phantasmagoria of being in love are actually negligible. Only those women able to understand this are ready for a peaceful conjugal life.

### Finding a Wife

What then do the motivations in the choice of a spouse reveal in such a context? What remains of the homogamy so vaunted by sociologists studying couples and Jean-Claude Kaufmann's assertion that "anybody doesn't marry just anybody: birds of a feather flock together"? It is true that also in Africa people often continue to marry individuals belonging to the same social group (class, culture, region, and so forth) as themselves. South African president Nelson Mandela fired the collective imaginary by taking as his third wife Graça Machel, the widow of the ex-president of Mozambique, Samora Machel. President Omar Bongo of Gabon didn't let scruples get in his way when he married the daughter of his neighbor and friend, President Denis Sassou Nguesso of the Congo.

But this general rule must be adjusted to the nihilism in love that is now to be seen everywhere. Everyone does not have the latitude available to King Mswati III of

Swaziland: on September 1, 2008, a crowd of more than thirty thousand young virgins gathered before his palace in Ludzidzini. Bare-breasted, they danced for more than an hour to allow him to choose his fourteenth wife. American humorist Jay Leno stated that such an event would be impossible in the United States, where there aren't thirty thousand virgins to be found . . .

The static and deterministic character of theories of endogamy is demolished by new morals of conjugality. A great many people marry taking into account criteria quite different from geographic proximity, cultural identity, or a shared social class. Thus couples are formed between partners who do not live in the same country, who are from different social groups or do not have the same level of education or share the same culture. A well-known example is Cameroon's president, Paul Biya who, after being head of state for more than a decade, took as his second wife a nice single mother more than thirty years younger than he, not only from a different ethnic group but with a rather scandalous reputation. Some of his compatriots took offense at this choice, seen as seriously damaging the honor of the Republic. Local newspapers tried to outdo each other in indignation, with front-page stories reporting sordid details of the previous love life of the new First Lady. As for me, I saw it, on the contrary, as a rare proof of clear-headedness on the part of a man thus showing, in an unexpected way, that he was capable of putting aside the ego of a black king to invite a woman of humble origins to share his private life.

Some Africans also speak of "remote control marriages" to designate a new type of marriage arranged for émigrés living abroad too long, who seek the help of influential members of their families back home to find them wives. Workers with ordinary jobs, but also executives with impressive careers in France, England, Belgium, Italy, Germany, and the United States thus resort to the help of their relatives (generally a mother, or the most respected aunt or uncle) to find the kindred spirit who will suit them, and use the necessary ingenuity and sense of diplomacy to coordinate the various stages of marriage (from organizing the flirtation to the negotiation of the contract and official and traditional ceremonies). Many Malians, Senegalese, and Ethiopians living abroad thus delegate the responsibility of the choice of their wives to relatives living thousands of miles away, but in whom they have full confidence. This approach is actually only an updating of "traditional" processes by which the love life and formation of a couple were formerly organized. It is all the more enduring in some émigré communities in that the culture shock in the host country is violent, assimilation difficult, and daily life in exile painful.

The ability of some African émigrés to detach themselves from the demands of conjugal love is actually somewhat reminiscent of the story of Wakefield, Nathaniel Hawthorne's hero. Saying he was taking a short trip, a man one day leaves his home without really knowing what he wants or even where he's going. With an enigmatic smile, he tells his wife that he shouldn't be gone too long. As she's always found him a bit mysterious, she doesn't ask too many questions. The man leaves. After taking only a few steps, he wonders why he should go farther. Without really knowing what's happening to him, he takes lodgings in a hotel on the next street, where he stays a day, a week, a year . . . Vaguely disguised, he lives anonymously for twenty years, without attracting the attention of his wife and friends, whom he sees almost every day. During this unpremeditated absence, he sees his wife grow older, but doesn't attempt to approach her. He himself socializes with no one, content to walk about from time to time without understanding what's happening to him. One day, rain forces him to take shelter right in front of his home. Without thinking, he opens the door wearing his habitual enigmatic smile, goes in, settles down, and takes up his life again right where he left off two decades earlier . . .

There is nonetheless an important difference between African émigrés living their conjugality by proxy during their long years of exile, and Wakefield's indecipherable casualness that cannot be explained by obvious psychological motivations. His story moves and disturbs the reader precisely because of the strangeness of his attitude, the impossibility of explaining the reasons for his actions, his fantastic ambiguity, and the inherent incoherence in his behavior that drives him in unexpected directions. For the African exiles, marriage is a rigorously codified ritual, an important calling with absence as the condition of its fulfillment. For Wakefield, it's a long, mysterious conversation whose language is often impossible to understand.

## The Memory of Oppression

The ways in which these new African families are formed is intriguing enough to make one want to know more about the ethics of conjugality and the dynamics of relationships within the couple. The monographs of anthropologists and sociologists on conjugal life in Africa abound in the results of surveys and polls, and in evidence indicating the very high degree of dissatisfaction in African households and the frustration of women who seem to consider themselves dominated, crushed both by the man's power and by the weight of the prerogatives accorded these "heads of family" by society. This literature poses the more general problem of "black masculinity" about which feminists constantly express their indignation. How can it be that, on one hand, women completely accept the new criteria regarding the choice of spouse and reject the sentimentalism of a superficial conjugal love while, on the other hand, complaining of how badly they are treated in marriage? What's behind this paradox?

First possible explanation: the instruments of empirical analysis used by researchers may fail to identify the true dynamics in play, either because the studies in question are conducted superficially, or because the surveys and polls do not succeed in identifying the extent of nontruth in the responses of people polled—statisticians have not yet invented techniques enabling them to measure deliberate lies.

Second hypothesis: African women may be less unhappily married than the social sciences suggest. First, because happiness is not necessarily a thing one is conscious of and that one conceptualizes for surveys, but above all because disillusionment leads them to commit voluntarily to relationships from which they do not expect the syrupy sentimentalism sought by anthropologists and sociologists. When they do detect it, for that matter, researchers interpret it simply as cynicism. Now it so happens that many women in Africa opt for a common-sense attitude: to them "love is shared egoism" (Antoine de La Sale).

That said, the heavy legacy of the oppression of women in the social history of mentalities, mores, and practices should not be neglected or minimized. Conjugal dynamics south of the Sahara are obviously part of the process of several centuries of double sexual and racial domination seen throughout the black world. Édouard Glissant reminds us of the painful genesis of the couple in Martinique in the context of slavery: "The 'family' in Martinique was at first an 'anti-family'. The coupling of a woman and a man to profit a master. It is the woman who muttered or cried: *Manjé tè pa fè yich pou lesclavaj;* the earth to be sterile, the earth to die. It is the woman who thus sometimes refused to bear in her womb the master's profit. The history of the family institution in Martinique is driven by this refusal. A history of an enormous primordial abortion: speech suppressed with the first cry."[7]

This original violence that marked the birth of the family is also put forward to explain the conjugal crisis in African American communities. "I think part of the problem is deep down in our psyche," asserts Cornel West. "The very notion that black people are human beings is fairly new in Western civilization and still not widely accepted in practice. And one of the consequences of this pernicious idea is that it is very difficult for black men and women to remain attuned to each other's humanity."[8]

The conditions of the emergence of the so-called modern family in the black world were in fact those of a social life organized around norms set by the oppressor and of a fragmented existence for each of its members: the "father" as slave in sugarcane fields or at hard labor; the "mother" as domestic help, broodmare of the future labor force and satisfier of sexual fantasies; and the "child" as a guarantee of free labor. This process of deliberate *nuclearization* of the African family was begun by the colonists and continued by the governments that succeeded the various independence movements according to the developments of the world economy. Such a process of dehumanization contributed to the mutual distrust and contempt that still today govern the relationships of couples in the black world.

Free oneself of self-hatred, extricate oneself from the snare of frustrations accumulated over several generations, rehumanize the way in which one considers one's conjugal partner: those were some of the ethical preoccupations of the Negritude movement. Léopold Sédar Senghor expressed their essence in a famous poem:

Naked woman, black woman
Clothed with your color which is life, with your form
    which is beauty!
In your shadow I have grown up; the gentleness of your
    hands was laid over my eyes . . .
Naked woman, dark woman
Firm-fleshed ripe fruit, somber raptures of black wine,
    mouth making lyrical my mouth . . .
Naked woman, black woman
I sing your beauty that passes, the form that I fix in the
    Eternal,
Before jealous fate turn you to ashes to feed the roots of
    life.[9]

Things have changed quite a bit, however. The memory
of the oppression of women within the black world remains alive but many are now emancipating themselves
from it. Refusing to continue to let themselves be tied by
the chains of history, they are coming out of the "enormous primordial abortion" spoken of by Glissant by
approaching conjugal life no longer as victims, but as
conquerors. They want to go beyond the innumerable
frustrations endured by their mothers and grandmothers
by freeing themselves of the illusion of love, this love too
often sought out of weakness or vanity. They believe that
genuine love is above all else self-esteem.

This philosophical approach is not new: African
women who scorn the desire to be loved and disdain the
escapades of sentimentalism could reconnect their view

of conjugality with that which determined the distribution of roles between spouses in their society before the European invasion. According to historian Gloria Chuku, "the colonial administrators came to Nigeria with western gender stereotypes. Their treatment of Nigerian women was based on ideas about 'women's fragility and dependence'. Western education was intended to produce good wives and mothers, and to enable women to run affairs at home, as the role of women was considered to be in the domestic sphere. In traditional Igbo society, however, the concept of a full-time housewife was unknown, and in the colonial period, Igbo women continued to operate outside the domestic sphere, as before."[10]

Her analysis is corroborated by the observations of G. J. Dei, who studied the behaviors of women in the villages of Ghana, and by various other studies devoted to the economic distribution of roles in African couples. Within families women thus have their own cycles of rights and duties, notably taking on the responsibility of food production and the education of children, while men attend to less "noble" occupations. So by reconnecting with the order of values of their precolonial societies, the women of Africa seem to have found the path to emancipation, and the means of reconquering their place on the social scene and the moral leadership that forces men's respect. In doing this, they do not, however, entertain illusions as to the supposed delights of conjugal life: opinion surveys show that their wardrobes are far more important to them than their sex life—as good a way as any to live nihilism.

## Truths of Orgasm

Visual representations are good indicators of how African women feel, not only about sexuality and their conception of power, but more generally about their relationship to authority, matters of social class, relations between the various age groups in society, and above all about new ways of defining their identities. The film *Les Saignantes (The Bloodettes)* by Cameroonian Jean-Pierre Bekolo illustrates this nicely. In the opening scene, you see a young woman making torrid, acrobatic love with an elderly man, who is none other than the secretary-general of the Civil Cabinet. Under the stress of pleasure and the young woman's sexual audacity, his heart soon gives out. Very briefly stunned, the woman quickly comes back to her senses, which she had for that matter never really left, and seeks the help of one of her friends to get rid of her victim's body—not, by the way, before relieving him of his money. The film is a wild, nocturnal chronicle of this adventure in a generously depraved world.

The artistic and technical qualities of this feature-length film have been discussed, as are almost all African cinematographic productions generally made with small budgets and asserting aesthetics different from those to which Western criticism is accustomed. What is striking in this satiric fable, supposedly taking place around the year 2025 in Yaoundé, is the change in the conceptions African women have of themselves. Long victims of their sanitized images and their perpetual fragility, they were reduced to the rank of sex objects on the fringes of history. They were thus useful only as subjects of anthropological studies. Weighed down by the feigned or real compassion of ethnologists, they were left to the commiseration of right-thinking humanity and became trade staples of feminism and Africanism. Films like *Faat Kiné* or *Moolaadé* by the Senegalese director Sembène Ousmane ratified this Manichean reading of the man-woman relationship in Africa, keeping alive in women's minds the idea that they were second-class citizens because they were incapable of using wickedness to their advantage. This classic image of the African woman as a prisoner of male desires and lacking self-confidence in the matter of sexual pleasure is now outdated.

In *Les Saignantes*, sexuality is thus not simply expressed as one of those elements of biopower that fascinated Michel Foucault. It is above all an element for expressing the truth about what one would like to be, about the type of social positioning to which one thinks one has the right. In this sense, it is the element that enables a woman to project the image of herself that she wishes to establish. It is an essential component of an assumed identity. It thus partakes of concern for oneself, self-subjectivation. We are here far from the questions generally discussed by political philosophers pondering sexuality: analytics of the modes of domination, discourse on the physiological organization of the body, significance of sexual orientations and behaviors, and so forth. Who would have thought that nearly illiterate African semiprostitutes would so creatively renew certain fundamental problematics of political economy?

Speaking of sexuality in Africa and the black world nevertheless remains a sensitive exercise: the subject is

often muddied by fantasies and myths created and peddled by the ethnopolitical mythology dating from the
time of the slave trade and the memory of oppression. It
is therefore not easy to propose a reading of behaviors
that avoids hasty generalizations. The double pitfall of voy-
eurism and clichés must be avoided, and a middle ground
found between the *racialist* discourse fueling Western collective fantasies about "black sexuality" and the reduc-
tionist and self-flagellating discourse of many African authors concerned with "political correctness." Cornel West
reminds us that in America collective sexual obsession
exists side by side with fear of black sexuality. This taboo,
however, must be broken and the subject demythologized
in order to open a constructive conversation on racism.

African public discourse on sexuality is fraught with
hypocrisy as well. On one hand, society claims to value
an ethical corpus that makes the subject taboo. Sexuality
is presented above all else as the medium of procreation.
It is reduced to marriage and conjugal duties and is clothed
with great spiritual significance. The state preaches sexual
austerity and laws are passed permitting the authorities
to interfere in the private lives of its citizens. There is also
an official distrust regarding pleasures deemed uncon-
ventional and an emphasis on their corrosive effects on a
person's soul and destiny. This results in a collective
anxiety about anything that can be considered as an
unacceptable democratization of "unnatural" sexual
practices.

On the other hand, there is a frenzied cult of the za-
niest sexual practices, which are even invested with mys-

tical virtues. Orgasm has its truths that the law does not know. Collective fantasies center on the sophistication of the techniques of sexual pleasure. This leads to an infatuation with pornography, one of those business activities where it seems difficult to go bankrupt. The Cameroonian cartoonist Popoli reports that those of his comics the public is most eager to get hold of are those that tell the raciest sex stories. Wolinski[11] would probably corroborate this remark.

In actual fact, African societies' authoritarian attempts at moralization through regulation of sexual activity reflect the sexualization of politics and the politization of sex. Sex is instrumentalized as a tool of selection, exclusion, and domination, as a medium of affirmation of identity (by women) and authority (by men). Sexuality is thus frequently a passport to the upper echelons of the administrative ladder or to wealth. In the prevailing order of values, homosexuality is often vigorously condemned. Curbed by the law, it is considered a sign of moral inferiority contrary to "African traditions" and to social norms. As was formerly the case with sexism, homophobia is actually used to exorcise the fear of this other hidden within ourselves. It almost serves as a "condom" to protect a certain conception of virility.

But one needn't be homosexual to use one's anatomy as a means of social affirmation. In those countries where heterosexuality is established as the official mode of sexuality, political and religious leaders of all kinds, intellectuals, and executives publically preach asceticism and abstinence. One must, they say, forgo the pleasures of the flesh. They are careful, however, not to apply their precepts to themselves. In accordance with unwritten social practice and norms known to everyone, a man with any self-respect has several wives—polygamy being recognized by the law—or at least several mistresses. The press regularly reports that to have a successful career in some firms, many young women must submit to the sexual fantasies of their superiors. These things are so commonplace that they no longer cause scandal or indignation. In universities and secondary schools as well, a great many female students flirt shamelessly with their instructors and, as if by chance, often get the best grades on exams. This, incidentally, doesn't prove a thing: perhaps instructors are interested only in the most naturally brilliant students? . . .

Exalting the pleasures of the body is, moreover, not limited to teachers and noisy elites cruising down the rut-filled streets of Douala or Kinshasa in big cars while listening to Mozart sonatas. It can be seen as well among the lower classes, who use it to escape everyday life, keep destitution at bay, and invent a different world for themselves. The general conditions of material poverty seem incompatible with the official culture of asceticism. They appear to justify hedonistic behaviors. The glorification of orgasm almost seems to be a kind of collective philosophical ambition: it's a matter of recognizing the unavoidability of suffering and death, of savoring the happiness of having thumbed one's nose at them and of achieving nirvana every day as best one can. What better than this "voluptuous death in life"? (Emil Cioran).

# 2

---

# I EAT THEREFORE I AM

## PHILOSOPHY OF THE TABLE

> Some men pursue pleasure with such breathless
> haste that they hurry past it.
>
> —SØREN KIERKEGAARD

> What is exhilarating in bad taste is the aristocratic
> pleasure of giving offense.
>
> —CHARLES BAUDELAIRE

At regular intervals, African "easy listening" music offers its public a hit tune that's often insipid, with an underlying insistent, binary beat, lacking harmonic subtleties but anchored in a vaguely charming melody and the hoarse screeching of a vocalist singing off-key without seeming to be bothered by it in the least. In that, its texture is quite similar to French and American easy listening music. In New York as in Paris, the essential criterion of "popular" bad taste seems to be its ability to mimic collective vertigo, not to express its subtleties. But in Abidjan or Kinshasa, hit songs exacerbate emotions and stir up crowds because they sometimes have a satiric dimension that give them a certain authenticity—an ability to capture the atmosphere of the times—and even an ethical pretention.

The success of the song "Antou" by the Ivory Coast group Magic System is due essentially to its ambition to synthesize the dominant features of the popular morality of the moment. It tells the story of a young woman who selects her lovers according to the sole criterion of purchasing power. Thus she sometimes makes a faulty analysis, as when she abandons a young singer who's in love with her but hasn't a penny to his name for a wealthier man. When she learns that the musical career of her ex-lover is unexpectedly taking off, she desperately tries to get him back. Wise to her, the young man takes her out to dinner, promising they'll have braised caiman and elephant kédjénou, imaginary spectacular dishes . . . He thus makes fun of her eating habits, which he likens to the desire to appear to be what she is not. The song's well-known refrain, chanted by children in the poor neighborhoods of large sub-Saharan cities, is as follows:

> I say sweet darling what do you want to eat
> Without even hesitating, she says braised chicken meat
> I say sweet darling, it's chicken you want to eat,
> Chicken is too small, that can't make you replete,
> It's braised caiman that you're going to eat
> Elephant kédjénou that I'll give you for a treat
> She's angry, she says, and she goes home . . .

No one can accuse the authors of this text of having produced great literature. But the song poses an interesting philosophical question: Is eating an innocent act? Not for Antou, the heroine of the story, nor for a great many Africans who didn't need to read Emil Cioran to become aware of the subliminal dimension of each meal. Before emigrating to France, the author of *All Gall Is Divided* had always "nourished himself like an animal, unconsciously, without paying attention to what eating means." In Paris, where he lived in a little hotel in the Latin Quarter, he saw the manager, his wife, and son get together every morning to decide on the menu of the meal; "they prepared it as if it were a battle plan!" That's when he understood that "eating is a ritual, an act of civilization, almost a philosophical statement."[1]

What does Antou teach us in her philosophy of dining menus? She reminds us first that in all human societies consumption patterns have, at all times, been potent symbols of power. What one eats and, more generally, what one consumes defines if not what one is (and the place one occupies on the social ladder), at least what one aspires to be. She also makes us aware of the various ways of conceptualizing questions regarding eating. A first method prevailing in the social sciences is inspired by the critique of a society of consumption and consumerism, and consists in analyzing the political economy of production and distribution by questioning the motives of the various actors and the power relationships among them. This is the approach—often Manichean—generally adopted by many geographers and sociologists of hunger, nutritionists and microeconomists. Another way of proceeding would consist in focusing, like Roland Barthes, on the modes of elaborating the values and rites of power that relationship to food reveals. Antou's story offers the opportunity to explore the nihilism of the sensual pleasure that can be seen in African table manners.

## Civilize through Sensual Pleasure

Any reflection on the significance of eating and, more generally, the economics of cultural day-to-day experience quickly comes up against the views of some anthropologists and sociologists. Based on an empirical study conducted particularly within Indian communities of Latin America, Lévi-Strauss, for instance, has explained the sometimes invisible systems of internal coherence that explain consumption habits. He certainly describes and interprets with a great deal of intuition the logical systems and alimentary functions and prohibitions and their justifications, the problems of compatibility and incompatibility, and so forth. He emphasizes the rules—at times unwritten—set by every society as to the rituals and management of matters concerned with eating, and as to submission to a certain world order that can be perceived in them. His conclusion: cooking "is a language in which each society encodes messages that enable it to signify at least a part of what it is."[2]

But his analyses read as if they were meant to be etched in stone and often present us with societies whose social order seems unchanging and whose actors are almost always passive. It is as though each eating pattern had its place on the predetermined register of a "normal" order of things. But like every medium of self-expression, the language of food is also an instrument of social organization, and is continuously subject to questioning and adjustment. It is thus less stable than Lévi-Strauss believes. Antou's story highlights this: in Abidjan or Kinshasa, alimentary practices are very consciously laden with significance. Certain things are eaten in certain places, at certain times, and in a certain way in order to express clearly to the world the manner in which one defines oneself and how one would like to be seen and treated. There is a voluntarism in the choice of what one eats and how one does it that stands in sharp contrast to the static observations that satisfy anthropologists.

Pierre Bourdieu has put forward a more dynamic analysis of this question, insisting on the stratification of society into social classes and on the idea of an aesthetics of bourgeois taste opposing the supposed vulgarity of lower-class taste. However, Antou's behavior prompts us to avoid any kind of Manicheism. In Africa, more than anywhere else, the boundaries of social groups are porous and uncertain. A systematic opposition of the eating practices of the middle class and the poor often does not work, since it is unstable: everyone strives (or is forced on some occasions) to display the same consumption habits. A poor young woman will not hesitate to ask for high-status braised chicken, to eat like the bourgeois, if only for one evening. And too bad if her lover of the moment snickers as he suggests braised caiman or elephant kédjénou . . .

What is more, the factors determining what one eats in each society vary greatly, for they sometimes have as much to do with necessity (climate and geography) as with tradition (history and culture). Much about them remains irrational and mysterious. It should also be noted that consumption habits are expressed in the context of an ever-evolving cultural core. The rice that today seems like the basic meal in a large part of Sahel Africa was introduced there less than a century ago. The bread that the Bantu populations of Central Africa consume daily as if it were an integral part of their most distant imaginary dates only from the colonial period. The same is true of the whiskey and champagne that now complete and validate some of the most important rituals in African cosmogonies.

Eating has thus never been an ordinary, meaningless act. In all times and places, humans have always conferred on this physiological need a symbolic importance and an almost metaphysical significance. A medium of social interaction and at the same time a setting for the redefinition and validation of individual and collective identities, the act of eating has always been an occasion when families and social groups exchange signs of complicity and ways of deciphering power relationships in the prevailing social order. This act obviously takes on a particular significance in regions of famine and poverty. In those cases, food choices and the way in which they are experienced and accepted become a luxury that one cannot always afford. In the same way, refusing to eat or depriving oneself of certain kinds of food also conveys diverse cosmogonies and social moral codes.

In Africa where millions of people go to sleep famished every night, eating is not only a biological imperative. In those countries where scarcity dominates the social imaginary, it is a moment of deliverance and pleasure. Eating is also a way of participating in the techniques of self-valorization, that is, implementing and negotiating one's relationship with oneself and others. It is thus, in the final analysis, a socially instituted mode of self-knowledge, a formulation of subjectivity. Beyond simple strong appetite, the act of eating can therefore be analyzed as one of the *aphrodisia* (acts, gestures, and contacts that give pleasure) sought after by the Greeks and Romans.

The sites and rituals of alimentation also reveal civilizations' codes of ethics. *Eating* can thus take an intimate, private form, permitting the head of a family to structure the dialogue and relationships within the household (man-woman, parents-children, and so forth). It can also take a semiprivate form, offering members of a social group the opportunity to interact on trivial or sensitive and serious subjects, but in a friendly atmosphere tempered by the organization of the dialogue around the ritual of a meal and drinks specially prepared to modulate tensions. It can, finally be expressed in a public form where eating is transformed into a veritable banquet, and where what is actually consumed is less important than the symbolism of the meal itself, the quality of the menu, the identity and social rank of the guests, the formality of the venue, the seriousness of the ambiance, the kind of music embellishing the occasion, and so forth.

In his contribution to *A History of Private Life,* Paul Veyne points out that from the days of the Roman empire the banquet has been considered a ceremony of civility. It was an occasion for a private man to savor what he was and to show it to his peers. "The banquet was more than just a meal. Guests were expected to express their views on general topics and noble subjects or to give summaries of their lives. If the host had a domestic philosopher or tutor on his staff, he would be asked to speak. Between dishes there might be music (with dancing and singing), by professional musicians hired for the occasion. [The classical banquet was] at least as much a social manifestation as an occasion for eating and drinking."[3] The banquet was thus used to assert oneself in the family or personal sphere, while at the same time offering the public man an opportunity to define himself in the eyes of his peers.

The same considerations can be found in the bourgeois rites of nineteenth-century France: having a meal was not only eating, it was creating happiness. Madame Celnart's *Manuel des Dames* (1833) illustrates this: "It is not only when one has guests that one should take care over the honors of the table. It should be done for one's husband, to civilize the home. I use this word advisedly; for what distinguishes civilization is to confer upon our needs a character of pleasure and dignity to the satisfaction of all."

In point of fact, the mystique of food consumption is often linked to reducing the dignity deficit one feels, and to individual and collective assertion of identity. Empirical studies devoted to consumption decisions in various regions of the world confirm this: consumption habits change with an increase in revenue, and express a certain concern for oneself. The wealthier a society becomes, the more nutrients its populations consume and the more the sources of these nutrients change. Econometric estimations of the demand for food and nutrients in northern China show, for example, that the allocation of food expenses changes considerably as household revenue rises. The nutritional importance of grains diminishes progressively in favor of more expensive food products like meat. The same change in tastes and food preferences has been seen in India, where studies show that populations are abandoning the consumption of grains in favor of the consumption of dairy products and meat as their standard of living increases.

Nutritionists and economists can be satisfied with these findings. The philosopher must attempt to discover their meanings and the ethical discourses expressed in the aesthetics of the table. Of course the changes observed in the structure of food expenditure do not merely reflect an increase in standard of living. They also correspond to a general change in alimentary habits throughout the world and in all social classes. The standardization of menus and table manners that can be noted by following the rate of increase in the number of McDonald's restaurants across the planet at least partly expresses this general Westernization of taste and culture. But beyond sociological considerations, alimentary choices are basically vehicles of meaning.

In the regions of the world where lack of food is a daily source of humiliation, what one eats is often a powerful vehicle of self-assertion and a symbolism of power. Cameroonians speak of "stomach politics" to designate the perception, in the collective subconscious, of individual strategies of accumulation and social positioning, of modes of access to institutions of domination—and thus of self-legitimation. What one eats partakes of a culture of power and expresses an ethos of munificence at the same time as a ritual of belonging to a relational network. Antou, the good heroine of the song, has no reason to be ashamed of the ethical ambitions she exhibits through her alimentary tastes, and which elicit her young lover's sarcasm: her choices express a philosophy of self-esteem and a quest for dignity.

## Aesthetics of Pleasures and Social Epicureanism

The aesthetics of the pleasures of eating are also connected with places and circumstances. One must have attended a banquet organized on the occasion of a "society" wedding in Douala or Yaoundé to assess this symbolism of having and being. These events, which regularly attract the attention of all the country's top executives in the private sector, the administration, and the government, generally take place on a Saturday evening and constitute the apotheosis of a process of celebration that sometimes spreads over a period of several weeks. Splendor, pomp, and luxury define not only the "success" or "failure" of the ceremonies, but also the place the married couple and their families intend to occupy on the social ladder.

When they don't put most of their savings into it, families generally go into debt to organize these dinners to which people go as much to see and watch as to be seen and admired. So for both the organizers and the guests, preparations begin far in advance. The venue is meticulously chosen, for it should reflect the importance and solemnity that the families want to confer on the event. The country's largest banquet halls are therefore requisitioned: a wedding dinner in the jet set is not considered a "success" unless it takes place in the grandiose Palais des Congrès conference center or at the Hilton Hotel, the most luxurious in the country.

A detailed program of the evening is generally drawn up, printed on glazed paper and distributed with the Bristol board invitation cards. As for the most funereal official ceremonies, it generally gives precise times of arrival for the different categories of guests. The most prestigious are generally accommodated in a special reserved space around the head table where the couple and their families will be seated. Those are usually Minister What's-His-Name, General So-and-So, the local billionaire, or the *Feyman,* the rich criminal who's the latest rage and whom everyone loves to talk about. The degree of prestige accorded to each of these personalities has to do with his power of influence and his supposed affluence—not with any moral and social leadership he may have.

Groomsmen and bridesmaids all dressed alike in outfits especially created for the occasion welcome the guests and usher them to the tables reserved for them. Each table has about ten place settings—Limoges porcelain and Christofle sterling for the poshest weddings—so that the guests can converse, as well as a selection of the best brandies for the aperitif. The banquet hall is often decorated in the colors of the groom's or bride's family—priority is given to the wealthier family, regardless of the usual considerations linked to tradition or lineage. In fact, in the course of preparatory meetings preceding these great ceremonies, intense negotiations take place between the representatives of the two families to determine which will have the longer list of guests or will finance the principal events of the evening.

In order to give the celebration all possible formality, professional hosts (television presenters, humorists, and well-known artists) are sometimes hired to enliven the evening. The dinner is then interrupted at intervals by entertainment and skits created to amuse and relax the audience and showcase the merits of the families involved in the marriage. Games of chance like lotteries and other drawings are routinely held in the course of the dinner, to distribute gifts to a few lucky people.

When the guests are all seated—which generally takes several hours because there are always a great many and they arrive in order between 8 P.M. and 1 A.M., according to the time given on the invitation—drinks are served: whiskey, champagne, or wine. Often one of the families has gone to the trouble of placing a special order of red wine or champagne from France, with its name printed on the labels . . . Thus one drinks bottles of Bordeaux wine labeled Château "Family X" and the year of the wedding date.

The meal is a solemn ritual. It begins with hors d'oeuvres that correspond neither to local eating habits nor even to the most widespread culinary tastes, but which people are mad about simply because of the prestige of their names: smoked salmon, caviar, and foie gras in the poshest circles; French-style salads with the most refined seasonings. Then come the hot courses, varied and abundant. Cheese from France, Holland, and Switzerland and desserts follow, the apotheosis being the famous wedding cake especially created by the best pastry chef of the area, and enjoyed with a good French champagne . . .

Toasts and speeches are part of the order of things. From time to time, a guest who's more excited than others takes the floor and revels in big words that seem to please the crowd. A speech to the glory of the couple and their families, or more or less funny jokes on the philosophy of love—whatever it is, people laugh and applaud, in a friendly atmosphere. It's all interrupted at intervals with carefully chosen musical renditions. Sometimes meetings are even held in advance simply to plan the running order of the musical compositions that embellish the diner.

Few guests are truly interested in classical music, the highlight of the evening. But all know its importance in such a context: it's the symbol of success. The guests thus almost religiously let themselves be lulled by Mozart adagios or the violin concerto by Beethoven, whose Ninth Symphony has been very popular since people have learned it's called the "Ode to Joy" . . . Fortunately, that never lasts very long: like a slightly boring intermission tolerated because it's part of an accepted ritual, the interludes of classical music are regularly interspersed with Cameroonian or Congolese songs. One thus passes without a transition from the languorous melodies of a seventeenth-century religious oratorio to the boisterous rhythms of the latest hard-driving Cameroonian *makossa* or the least romantic Congolese *ndombolo*. Handel and Monteverdi cohabit with Koffi Olomidé. And when the master of ceremonies tells the disc jockey: "Quick! Music for an eating ambiance! Something to give people an appetite!" one's reminded of Louis de Funès shouting in the middle of a meal in the movie *L'aile ou la cuisse (The Wing or the Thigh)*: "No, not Wagner! Wagner is for the dessert!"

This sort of wedding dinner is admittedly limited to the urban jet set. But even if everyone does not have the financial means for such extravaganzas, many in the less wealthy social classes try to reproduce this pattern. Even when they are simpler, with a reasonable menu and ordinary guests, the propensity to orgies is a social reflex among the needy. They too accord a definite philosophical significance to the locations and rituals of eating. In poor neighborhoods the rare feasts to which people can occasionally treat themselves are often a time to celebrate closeness and camaraderie and to exalt the collective self.

### Ethics and Moral Significance of Taste

Eating partakes of ethics and morality. There is a moral code of banquets and orgies; that is, a body of unwritten values and rules of action stipulated by social institutions (the family churches, the state) for citizens' private and public celebrations. This moral code of celebration tends, in turn, to give rise in each individual to ways of being and doing, "moralities of behaviors" that may be conscious or unconscious. Individual ethics is the way in which each citizen becomes integrated into the corpus of current prescriptions and freely becomes a moral subject of the larger social code. Antou's alimentary code of ethics illustrates this subjection and the way in which each citizen feels obligated to implement the system of social rules and values. This sub-Saharan African code of ethics which attempts to make of one's life a work of art has as its substance *aphrodisia* as well as desire, concupiscence, and the flesh. It is, nonetheless, not a blind submission to a moral code; it is a personal aesthetic and philosophical choice.

Eating is also an aesthetics of the self. In the African context, it is an act that casts light on several kinds of radically different moralities: a morality of deprivation that consists in conforming scrupulously to social rules and obeying the injunctions of those who decree what should be considered in all circumstances as the appropriate behavior; and a new sub-Saharan African morality centered on ethics and whose principle is to enjoy oneself by transforming one's life, constantly instilling it with aesthetic concern. The attitude of Antou, a rebellious young woman who rejects good upbringing, a good conscience, alimentary minimalism, and the censure of her tastes, represents an interesting problematization of the break between conflicting moralities. It also constitutes an attitude of modernity, in the sense that it expresses self-invention. "To be modern is not to accept oneself as one is in the flux of the passing moments," said Michel Foucault; "it is to take oneself as object of a complex and difficult elaboration."[4] It is to free oneself of the influence of the prevailing moral prescriptions and freely place one's action in one's own actuality. This inventive self-production does not, however, intend to reaffirm the pre-eminence of the sovereign, individualist subject. It is rather part of a process of subjection that is simultaneously autonomous and in solidarity with one's fellow citizens.

Certain tastes and savors are very precisely associated with a mental attitude or a moral code of character. Whereas in the West "sweetness," for example, has brought to mind moral judgments since the middle of the seventeenth century, south of the Sahara it rather tends to bring to mind a certain form of candor and immaturity, even weakness and naiveté. Thus those tastes and savors are "naturally" the province of women and children—it is fitting for them to consume in public only sweet beverages, even if they contain alcohol. The beverages prized by women are therefore generally fortified wines or imported liqueurs. The consumption of "strong" spirits, which include traditional or imported beer as well as exotic beverages like whiskey, is associated with the positive values of power, courage, and resistance. The consumption of "strong drink" is moreover generally accompanied by that of very hot dishes ("spicy"), symbols as well of power and virility. This combination of "strong" and "spicy" is, incidentally, a rite of passage to adulthood, the affirmation of an unquestionable virility, the admission into the big boys club. And when a woman dares to show an overly great inclination to consume strong liquor or spicy dishes, she is admired but also feared, and people wonder about the virility of her partner . . . In Cameroon people won't hesitate to ask him: "Who wears the pants at your house?"

Bubbly alcoholic beverages like sparkling wines and champagne disrupt this moral order somewhat because the formality associated with them transcends social categorizations and labels. They celebrate the joy of life and in principle everyone has a right to them. In accordance with the principle of the democratization of happiness, everyone is therefore permitted, for instance, to enjoy the good taste of this champagne that embodies an appetite for life—that cardinal value common to African societies. The sparkling bubbles seem to bear within themselves the effervescence and splendor of a life one would like to be as happy and dynamic as possible. The impetuous sound of the popping cork generally followed by a round of applause, the solemn transparency of this pure, refined alcohol—strong enough so it can't be gulped down and mild enough not to get the average person drunk on the first glass—the requirement to respect the proper temperature, for champagne must be drunk quite chilled; all this is part of a social ethic and a new ritualization of taste.

This collective craze for luxurious orgy does not prevent many citizens from cultivating other forms of distinction by opting for atypical behaviors. There are thus a growing number of vegetarians among African managers and executives—particularly those who have studied abroad. While there is nothing extraordinary about being a vegetarian in Kolkata, since that is part of the customs of a great many people, in Dakar or Douala it is still unusually stylish, enabling one to place oneself in the collective imaginary into the same category as myth- ical vegetarian figures like Confucius, Plato, Leonardo da Vinci, or Kafka. Some espouse religious beliefs and prac- tices recommending such a lifestyle, either from a need for intellectual exoticism or from a nihilistic concern for difference. Others conform to it chiefly because they wish to cultivate a public image of purity and sobriety that helps distinguish them more easily from the masses. And yet such efforts are not necessary: "We are sometimes as different from ourselves as we are from others" (François de La Rochefoucauld).

So, in the end, our good Antou understood it all: the hedonism exhibited by her tastes is above all else the medium of her struggle for dignity. Eating in a time of scarcity cannot be a neutral act. Beyond the demands of biology, it is also the means of expressing one's engage- ment in the battle of life, of clinging to existence, of proclaiming one's courage, of scoring a little victory— certainly provisional, but a victory all the same—against death; this death that prowls about with the frenzy and the patience of an angry debtor. Seen from this angle, the alimentary ambitions of the young woman are under- standable: it's not simply a question of the very general desire for distinction set forth by Pierre Bourdieu; be- yond the pleasure principle that is an essential dimension of the way of life in sub-Saharan Africa, her choices are also the expression of a struggle against failure, lack, and destitution. They enable her to pull herself up to where the important people are, into the social group of those who are respected. The message is clear: destitution will humiliate neither her dreams nor her unquenchable quest for dignity and respect. Her unreasonable tastes—if judged by criteria of economic rationalism—command not scorn, but admiration. Beyond their superficiality, they essentially convey a desire for self-affirmation and a need for recognition of the humanity of those who, like Fernando Pessoa's heroes, like to think that they are great in their souls despite their minute destinies.

# 3

## POETICS OF MOVEMENT

### VISIONS OF DANCE AND MUSIC

I like Congolese music: even when it's bad,
it speaks to the body.

—SONY LABOU TANSI

Without music, life would be a mistake.

—NIETZSCHE, *Twilight of the Idols*

Recollections of music and dance intoxicate my African memory. As far back as I can recall, the performance of movement has always ornamented my imaginary and marked out the field of my dreams. My mother did not merely entertain her children with lullabies: she would put the words into resonant forms and give them a visual and at times spectacular aspect that calmed the most rebellious soul. When she was cooking, she'd carefully watch the foods simmering in her saucepans and express her contentment in cadenced stamping around her stove, or by humming Congolese songs like "Kaful Mayay" by Tabu Ley Rochereau or "Makambo Mibale" by Les Bantous de la Capitale.

As for my father, his immoderate taste for life often expressed itself in unexpected explosions of unexplained, contagious joy. This was reflected in his propensity to prioritize physical expression, sometimes in public. In traffic jams, he'd give the hand brake a sharp pull and briefly leave the driver's seat of his vehicle to do a few dance steps in the middle of the street, as if the song playing on the radio produced unbearable itching in his body. Our neighbors in Douala, Yaoundé, Mbalmayo, and Akonolinga, had eventually gotten used to his nocturnal outbursts: without ever feeling guilty because it was midnight or 3 A.M., he'd open the windows to enjoy the hot night breeze, then pick up his old acoustic guitar and, between two swallows of beer, yell out a pagan melody in his hoarse voice accompanied by uncertain chords.

My parents weren't particularly whimsical. Even today their behavior would still be considered harmless in the black world, where dance and music compose the sonorous, aesthetic background of daily life. Not because "emotion is Negro, reason is Greek" as Léopold Sédar Senghor claimed in a surge of *negroism*. More simply because the musical arts often seem to us as obviously the best way to express our most intimate truths. It's not surprising that Socrates began to learn music on the day his death sentence was announced . . .

The insidious power of dance is fairly easily explained: it is the art closest to the experience of living. It therefore stimulates the human body more intensely than any other, and makes it move in reaction to its environment. It is also a theory of movement that enables one to communicate with others by a process of kinetic transfer, and, for instance, to strike up a silent but intense dialogue between dancer and audience.[1] This intimate exchange of mute remarks is sufficient unto itself.

The philosophical legibility of music is less obvious. Not only because of its nondiscursive, symbolic aspect, but above all because its language and the range of emotions it arouses are far more sweeping than the register in which words are expressed. Elvis Costello has warned those who venture to transfer a mode of artistic expression from the medium in which it was conceived into another: "Writing about music is like dancing about architecture—it's really a stupid thing to want to do." Plato suggested the same thing when he made distinctions between the intelligible and the sensible, the ideal and the artistic. He felt that music is the medium of another universe which is difficult to interpret.

Translating the subtleties and mysteries of music into words is certainly a perilous exercise. But the dichotomy suggested by Costello and Plato does not work very well in Africa where music is inseparable from the human condition. In Kinshasa or Abidjan, music is even too important a dimension of the current cosmogonies for thought to abdicate its role of critical interpretation. This role is all the more important today because, despite praise by from critics on the international artistic market, African dance and music continue to be the targets of discreet, recurrent contempt. A sign of this disdain: Western art critics almost always speak of them to emphasize their supposed Africanism—their "boisterous" rhythms, their "joyous" tonality, and their "colored" instrumentation—and rarely to praise their intrinsic musicality. They focus only on their nihilistic philosophies and most superficial aspects.

Three recollections come to mind that confirm the broad stylistic and philosophical range of African musical arts. The first is that of a recent Cameroonian ball in Toronto where the tireless movements of the dancers in a trance did indeed remind me of the sophisticated nihilism of the clientele of popular bars in Africa. The second is linked to the intensity of the aesthetic experience I felt listening to a recent album by the Congolese musician Lokua Kanza. The third is that of my first conversation with Cameroonian Richard Bona, whose work and artistic career reflect a refusal of the conformism and Epicureanism that people systematically want to attach to African music.

## Dance: A Nihilistic Prayer

First recollection: I'm attending the Toronto Cameroonian community's annual ball. By going there, I thought I was accepting a little invitation from friends who wanted to participate in a "little" gathering where hundreds of immigrants would get together to shed the anxieties of exile and the stress of urban life. I should have realized that the event wasn't ordinary: my host, an eminent film professor at the University of Toronto, extracted from the depths of his wardrobe a handsome beige summer suit. With a Borsalino fedora, you would have taken him for Robert Redford in *The Great Gatsby*. His wife spent most of the day in a hair salon with remarkable results. This insistence on elegance, incidentally, forced me to change the unobtrusive black suit I'd planned to wear for the occasion.

Several hundred families dressed to the nines crowd into the large hall rented for the occasion. They seem determined to celebrate the material well-being to which Canadian exile has given them the right, and the memories of that distant Cameroon they continue to feel nostalgic about, without for all that feeling guilty about its mediocre reputation. We were only about four hours late for the evening's announced program. No one dreamed of complaining about that: by Cameroonian standards, such a performance even got us dangerously close to trivial Swiss punctuality.

As always in Cameroonian celebrations, everything starts with a banquet—after all, the specter of famine menacing the collective imaginary must be warded off. The menu is rich in spicy dishes, in condiments from back home giving off the aromas of childhood. We eat quickly and well. Then, the evening's organizers are accorded their little moment of glory. The hired impresario hands them the microphone so they can indulge in a bit of self-promotion and promise to do even better in the years to come. Inaudible speeches that are loudly applauded in the happiness of seeing those who made them leave the stage and clear the way for serious things: dancing.

Scheduled to begin at 9 P.M., the ball finally opens at forty-seven minutes after midnight. It was high time: tired of waiting, many guests rush to the floor, too small to accommodate them all. No matter. Or so much the better, actually. The more they are crowded against each other, the more they appreciate the intensity of the moment. So they go to it with fervor. The music seems to infiltrate their bodies and show on their joyous faces. Two Canadian women lost in the crowd dance as wildly as they can to show they're up to the ambient frenzy. An anthropology of gestures would perhaps be able to decipher the mystical arabesques they trace in the air with their long arms. Everyone knows the songs. There's nothing transcendent about the lyrics, but the hall in frenzy sometimes takes up in chorus the most explicit words:

> Everybody's fucking crazy about you
> I'm fucking crazy about you
> We don't give a fuck about anything
> Frotambo! Frotambo! . . .

I have the impression my vision's getting blurry when I notice a pregnant woman right in all the movement in the middle of the floor. No, my eyes aren't playing tricks on me: she's really there, active, focused, light as air. The fact that she's almost full term doesn't diminish the degree of her excitement. She's singing and dancing with more energy than the others. I think of her future baby who, from the depths of its placenta, must be wondering what its upcoming life on earth will be like.

The music seems to provoke uncontrolled reflexes. It first attacks the rough edges of their bodies before stirring up all their impurities. It defies their stiffness and roundness, forcing them to the most daring movements and the most unexpected contortions. Women who were timid and stilted in their fashionable evening gowns are suddenly transformed into intrepid gazelles. Men one would have thought unfitted for sports turn out to be as nimble as cats, bounding, hopping, and stamping their feet more or less elegantly to the rhythm of the hoarse howls and moans coming from the speakers. I can easily picture them breaking a few records at the Olympics. The insistent beat of the bass drum in particular seems to draw from all these men and women their remaining bit of mystery. From their playful body movements—posteriors moving dangerously, hips swaying languorously, rubbing against each other, bumping into each other, big breasts teasing panting chests, avid gazes heavy with unconcealed pleasures, prying hands sometimes wandering below the belt—it's quite obvious that it awakens guilt buried in the depths of their souls. One senses, for that matter, that if the lights were turned out very different things would take place. For all these good citizens who pay their taxes and try to obey the laws, dancing permits them not only to pour out sweat but also to express all their bad thoughts, those shameful desires for violence and other things besides. It frees them from the insidious rancor hidden in the depths of their bodies. For the time of a song, it makes them peaceful outlaws, delinquents at liberty. Nihilism is there, quite present: the "bad desires," the shameful drives, the guilty cravings are not far away. Perhaps they actually constitute the secret of the celebration. After all, someone at my table tells me, they make existence bearable.

Their movements, for that matter, are like confessions: in a matter of a few seconds, I feel that I know a lot more about each of them than about the neighbors who live around me or the office colleagues whom I've been working alongside for years. A hurried observer would see in this spectacle only the cult of fleeting pleasures, the awkward expression of sexual urges, and the sometimes unsightly display of bodily desires. But these pagan dances are much more than a superficial form of hedonism. They are also a way of appropriating for oneself time that is passing, irrevocable time. Each second that disappears forever is an opportunity to aerate one's mind, to oxygenate one's brain, to subdue the death toward which it moves us inexorably. From the grins of enjoyment on their faces, I can see that, although physically just a few feet from me, they are in reality a thousand miles away, safe in an out-of-this-world where miracles take place: that of connecting with the intimacy of the other and finding oneself in unknown persons; or that of mastering the tempo of existence, of enjoying it immediately, though without the hope that such happiness will be accessible the next day. For they believe that pessimism and optimism are both signs of mental imbalance, and that the quest for good or evil is totally indefensible. Existence should be managed outside of all moral judgment, in the nocturnal fullness and intensity of each instant, in the here and now.

They're also dancing to leave their bodies and escape from lives that have remained poor despite material ease. They're dancing to escape a past that still has a hold on them beyond exile and success and permanently threatens to bring them back toward the horizon of destitution. They're dancing to vanquish bad luck. Their random body movements are thus in reality a nihilistic prayer: in refusing to submit to the linearity of movement, they invoke pagan gods who could offer them a world freed from the dictatorship of the inevitable, and a life where individual and collective destinies would not be predetermined. The race toward nothingness is here expressed in the form of a voluptuous celebration of a life outside of life, of an imaginary place where one situates oneself in order to ignore this imperfect and unbearable reality.

The fact that this dance music "speaks to the body" as writer Sony Labou Tansi said, does not, however, deprive it of its ambition to express a meaning. Through its nihilism, it also expresses an ethics of existence. The dancers are not interested in doing a philosophical reading of the songs coming out of the speakers, but simply in experiencing their incantatory power and *living* them fully. As I watch them I think of the ascetic nihilism of someone like Schopenhauer, a philosopher of the absurd and theoretician of the absence of happiness, stating that "life oscillates like a pendulum. From right to left, from suffering to boredom." He would be quite surprised to find how little these dancers think of his minimalist philosophy. On this evening in Toronto disillusionment does not express itself in the style of modesty and bitterness but rather in the mode of immoderation and excess. This nihilism has no need to be sickly and naïve. On the contrary, it couldn't care less about representations of boredom and evil and cultivates an Epicureanism without illusions. Life is worthless, but that is no reason for inflicting upon oneself the sacrifices of asceticism. Debauchery is thus a refined form of skepticism.

For a few others, dance is the vehicle toward emptiness, the means of dusting off one's soul, of forgetting oneself and attaining the Absolute. Elsewhere, some people reach it by disconnecting from the world, experimenting with the use of illegal substances, joining sects, or feeding on bitterness. That's the nihilism of anger. In Toronto's Cameroonian community, what is celebrated is rather the nihilism of vacuity. More refined, it consists in "making oneself absent to everything, plunging into the innermost depths of this absence, and purifying oneself there of all those stains that tarnish and clutter the mind. Freeing oneself and vanquishing oneself, acting dead with absolute consciousness, that is, empty of all contents, liquidating all mental heritage—for a quarter of an hour or for one minute."[2] They dance to rid their minds of the illusory dreams that weave the fabric of everyday life. They wriggle to reach the deep truth of each instant. Dancing helps them constantly remember that there's nothing to lose or win in life, nothing that's not fundamentally a mirage. Existence can then be organized appropriately. Leaving the hall in the early hours of dawn, I couldn't help thinking of this statement by Herbert Spencer: "Opinion is ultimately determined by the feelings, and not by the intellect."

## The Algebra of Mystery

The second recollection concerns the mystery of the aesthetic experience, and the feeling of being able to decipher sonorous allegories and images of another genre of African music—that of the Congolese Lokua Kanza. I'd awakened that morning with a larger dose of world-weariness than usual: no desire to do anything at all and very little energy to brave the twenty or so miles of gridlock leading from my Maryland house to my Washington, D.C., office. Some days are like that. I'd had to think hard about the activism engaged in every day by some of my "political adversaries" to find in my subconscious the strength to get out of bed and get ready to face the day.

On my way to the car, I nonetheless instinctively picked up a recording of new songs that Lokua Kanza had sent me. He'd told me he was still working on them and that this was far from the finished product. I'd scarcely put the disc into the player when I felt an electric jolt run through me. Instant miracle in my car and immediate transformation: gone was the mood of malaise and *untranquillity*. I was fluttering about. I could have said like Guy de Maupassant that I no longer knew if I was breathing music or hearing fragrances. I felt myself seeping into each guitar arpeggio and sanza note. I couldn't sit still. Like my mother at her stove, I hummed each tune at the top of my voice. Traffic jams and reckless drivers suddenly didn't matter. Actually, I pitied them because they did not, like I, have access to this music. A few minutes earlier I had the impression of being outside the world and stripped of my own life. And now, in the space of a few guitar chords, Lokua Kanza was bringing me back through the main entrance and relegitimizing the reasons for my existence.

When I got to the office, I continued to sing and dance (without music), this time comfortable in my petrol blue alpaca suit. My bureaucrat's tie didn't bother me in my movements. My Indian assistant, a good, honest mother as outrageous as Mother Teresa, had suddenly stopped drinking her tea to stare at me, wider-eyed than usual. Did she take me for the reincarnation of Shiva Nataraja, the cosmic dancer? I didn't pay any attention to her. I was in a trance. In a state of pure levitation, like the fakirs in Bollywood films. It was only when I sat down in front of my computer screen and saw the cascade of "urgent" messages that had arrived during the night and required all my attention that the spell broke: a monetary crisis expected in Ukraine, a new increase in the price of a barrel of oil threatening to seriously upset the balance of payments of a great number of countries, and statistical readjustments that spectacularly increased our detailed account of the number of poor people in the world . . . For the time being, I had to come back down to earth.

Lokua Kanza: music of melancholy, music of the intoxication of desire, music of faith, that sometimes makes one want to visit the beyond. Without sound or fury, it invalidates the tendency to dwell on the sordid side of life and the destitution too often associated with Africa. It speaks delicately of its nobility and dignity in dry arpeggios that mark out the notes and detach them so that the music itself detaches from them, and which strike the ear all the more easily because the rest of the orchestra often lets the acoustic guitar play alone—as if to offer it the maximal amount of oxygen. Here, each half tone, chromatic or diatonic and considered the smallest distance between two notes in Western music, is transformed into an infinite distance where the slightest sigh evokes the panting of the wind, and the most insignificant onomatopoeia resounds like one of those sensual groans heard only when walking in tropical forests. In the dusk of each note, a pernicious, insistent light. In the enigma of each interval, whether diminished, minor, major, perfect, or augmented, subtle melodies and delicate harmonies. Complexity of things said and not said and equivocal sensations. Congo, that faraway and sometimes fantastical country, has never been so near.

Above all, there's that dizzying voice, pirouetting while remaining centered, at once crystalline and dark, driven by an energetic melancholy. Warm and imperious when it descends, incandescent on the high notes, it is staggeringly sweet when it stops and its syllables continue to flow in the listener's subconscious. Its most innocuous inflexions express a cleansed anxiety, a purified pain. Yet nothing voluble. Just an unbearable clarity, an austere voluptuousness, a solemn peace, an atmosphere of prayer, a humble entreaty, a familiarity with the Eternal, a noble, tranquil fervor. With that bit of ecstasy in the phrasing, lunar and tormented, it encourages confession. Burning with sincerity, it would shake the coarsest soul and even convince a murderer to admit his crimes. Its intonations, tremolos, vibratos, and minor sonorities tell us something more than the words—something heralding, like improbable good news. To speak of optimism would be overstating the case. But one can reasonably evoke a somber hope, for this voice dispels obscurity and lightens silence. It intimidates darkness and allows the listener to feel his heart, to glimpse the dawn that we all bear within ourselves. It affords respite from nightmares and gives credibility to the idea of deliverance.

Delicately embroidered like confessions and confidences, Lokua Kanza's songs do not, however, have the simplistic sentimentalism of slogans/clichés. They are a chronicle of the "splendor of the existential impasse." Elegant in their sobriety, inventive in their mystery, and with an indwelling breath of liturgy, they make an algebra of unknown words familiar to us—words in Lingala that, scarcely pronounced, are immediately part of our respiration. Words that, behind their veil of modesty, send a gentle breeze adrift in our consciousness. We then have the feeling that the heavens are faintly smiling.

It's impossible after listening to something like this not to give in to the intoxication of the possible. Guitars, percussion, whispers of grief, murmurs of joy, poetics of a luminous sweetness. Yes, so much sublimity can only herald a new dawn. Even when, in fleeting moments, the insidious character of a harmonic leitmotif gives rise to a little twinge of sorrow, or when the legato of a melody diffuses a shiver of sadness, vertigo here is always rainbow-colored: bitterness permanently rubs shoulders with bursts of happiness. Mystery is always cleared up in the end and one understands that this prophetic voice brings us the good news: time belongs to us and there may, after all, be a beginning of meaning to life. Hope will no longer be a mere slogan. So the question arises: What has happened to the nihilism that's said to be consubstantial with Bantu music? Where is this "dance music" whose rhythms are supposedly driving millions of Africans around the world wild every day, from Douala to Toronto?

Perhaps, in the final analysis, Pierre Souvtchinsky is right: musical creation and its perception are above all else innate processes of intuitions organized around experimentation with time.[3] For each individual, time passes at a rate that varies according to the inner dispositions and the events that affect consciousness. It goes by at different durations depending upon whether one is subject to anxiety, boredom, pain, or pleasure, according to whether one is looking forward to something or simply in a state of uncertainty. The perception each individual has of music is determined by psychological processes, having their own tempos. These variations in psychological time are perceptible because they are, after all, related to the sensation—whether felt consciously or unconsciously—of real time, ontological time. Whether it conforms to the "normal" flow of time or dissociates itself from it, all music establishes a particular relationship between its own duration, the time that is passing, and the techniques through which it expresses itself. It is thus possible to distinguish two kinds of music: one which evolves parallel to the process of ontological time, inducing in the listener a feeling of euphoria and more easily inviting him to dance; and one which differentiates itself from this process, not limiting itself to tonal units, playing on instability to express the unexpected and the unforeseeable.

With Lokua Kanza, musical time varies from one composition to another: at times, it conforms to ontological time. Stylistic unity is then the fundamental principle. The intensity of the musical experience then simply shows in the repetition of the chief melodic lines. In other compositions, the persistence of the themes is accompanied by a harmonic profusion and a variety of contrasts, tonal colors, a multiplicity of atmospheres, and even by recourse to counterpoint; the listener is thus stealthily invited into experimentation with psychological time. In both registers, the simplicity of forms reflects far more than modesty in the selection of the elements of the music and the quality of the arrangements: it conveys above all the sincerity of its temperament. The gentleness of the orchestration and the choice of favoring the most burning emotion to the detriment of technical virtuosity bring out the musical density of a work whose elegance goes right the heart of things. Here music does not cheat: it has no need of artifice to be sensual and elegant.

In each creator's artistic career, there comes a special moment when, no longer needing to prove anything, he finds himself face to face with his own consciousness, freed of the imperatives imposed by the need to please or charm. It is a kind of equilibrium where the singularity of his identity reveals itself. This rare instant has the dark beauty of a lunar eclipse. The artist no longer appears as a producer of cultural material and becomes simply the transcriber of his sensations, the witness of the present time, the secretary of collective questionings, the faithful interpreter of his doubts. Lokua Kanza has reached such a point in his musical journey. His work is now a return to sources and to himself, a reflexive movement whose sobriety does not distort the truth. Even if he doesn't make his Congolese compatriots and the members of the African diaspora in Toronto and elsewhere dance, he constitutes that precious space where historians of the future will communicate freely and satisfy their thirst to understand a continent that is regularly referred to as timeless, outside of history, lost in its grief.

### The Precision of Chaos

The third recollection is that of my first conversation with Cameroonian jazz musician Richard Bona. That night he was appearing with Mike Stern in concert in Washington. We'd had lunch in a Georgetown café and spent the afternoon discussing today's African music, its vaguely demonic reputation, its new trends, and its aesthetics. I'd told him that some of his compositions were for me the source of a recurring emotion. And that each note, each chord, each inflexion of his voice seems to write a testament and be the last trace of a testimony destined to leave an indelible mark on the consciousness of the listener. Reminding him of François-Bernard Mâche's claim that "music serves to unjam neuronal circuits, which are intrinsically hard-wired for it," I'd explained that his work confirmed my idea that music is also an essential biological activity.

He'd looked at me with his sharp, penetrating gaze, and simply smiled as he sipped his big glass of soda and ate his chips. Then he'd acknowledged that those who attempt to understand his music by considering only its materiality confine the analytical work to which it invites the listener to an exercise in superficiality.

To grasp the essence of the antinihilistic feeling that characterizes his songs, one must explore their form attentively and decipher the creative process underlying them. His basic postulate is the simple idea that all music worthy of the name requires a certain degree of organization—and is thus a conscious act. Otherwise it is nothing but an insipid cacophony and an arbitrary revolt. Like Igor Stravinsky, he certainly considers that musical creation is above all else a speculative phenomenon, a succession of impulses and surges that delicately converge toward a point of serenity—the moment of tranquility and peace. But he does not ignore the lessons of several centuries of musical exploration and refuses to conform strictly to the rigidities of the diatonic system and the demands of classic tonality. His art of musical composition is far richer than the absolute value of the major-minor system dictated by the scale of middle C.

The insidious upheavals that Bona would like to inflict on musical topography do not, however, go so far as to destroy melody, whose status remains paramount for him. He knows that of all the elements of music, melody is perhaps the most precious, the one through which an immediate connection with the audience is established. He also knows that the ability to produce unforgettable melodies does not result from intellectual work but from a mysterious gift to which musicians of genius like Beethoven were not entitled. Melody is thus always at the heart of his musical alchemy, in whatever form he chooses to express himself. His approach to the art, for that matter, invalidates the usual discrimination between instrumental and vocal music: whichever medium he uses, melodic intensity and richness remain intact.[4]

He also told me that he didn't consider himself a revolutionary in music—he doesn't care for the kind of disorder that the idea of revolution implies. Rather, he positions himself as an aesthetical fundamentalist, a researcher and an innovator. Several factors motivate such positioning. First, his personal and spiritual journey: one is not born with impunity in this Africa that is ashamed of its postindependence; one does not come unscathed out of a life made contingent by arbitrariness and evil; one could not therefore be a conformist when each cherished childhood memory is marked with scars of sorrow and violence (he'd shown me the top of his head where his father left a huge lump shattering the first guitar he'd been forbidden to play). In that Africa, music all too often mimes angst and the social upheavals of the moment, and is reduced to a mere utilitarian vulgate accompanying the movement in vogue. It is then a form of nihilism offered to the lower classes either to titillate their lower instincts or to caress their minute desires for pleasure. But from the very beginning of his career, Bona had chosen to position his work in reaction to the big national hubbub, against the reduction of music to an instrument of social moralizing, and against the petty use of art to maintain stable imbalances.

Next, his artistic journey: although he was born in the immense equatorial forest and started his career in the extravagant disorder of what is called African easy listening music, Bona was raised on jazz as others are on mother's milk or the bottle. The fact that he largely educated himself, wanting to be as good a bassist as Jaco Pastorius, only stimulated his desire for the unusual and his constant concern to durably enrich his technique. His emotional journeying between Douala, Paris, and New York—places where music lovers are not content to enjoy a creative work from the outside but insist on verifying its essence—grounded his approach to musical composition. Critics who listen to his work superficially simply call him "inspired." One must examine it seriously and study, for instance, the scores of his songs to understand that the "inspiration" that does indeed emanate from his repertoire is certainly obvious but is actually a secondary aspect of the creative process. What is essential is rather his obsession with balance, symmetry, and measure—that is, in the final analysis, with how little is left to chance.

Bona obviously trusts his inspiration, but is wary of it and "manages" it with the rigor and precision of the traditional big game hunters of eastern Cameroon where he grew up. The lessons of life and of musical technique that he has amassed throughout his journeying across several continents have convinced him that musical creation cannot be limited to something as fortuitous and arbitrary as an inspired melody. It must, on the contrary, be a complex chain of labor guided and put into harmonious order by instinct. To be credible, instinct must be backed by technical knowledge and validated by work. In the difficult voyage that constitutes the process of creation, the idea that inspiration alone is enough to reach perfection is simply a hoax. The natural gifts of melodic invention should not merely submit to the caprices of the imaginary. They should be exploited and evaluated critically to enable the artist to overcome and magnify chance. Like Stravinsky, he believes that "the more art is controlled, limited, worked over, the more it is free." Musical creation is a somewhat disorderly art. But the process becomes an artistic product worthy of this name only if it is mastered. A composer who wants to leave a mark on posterity must remain the master of his emotions and his imaginary. He must set his sights on the precision of chaos.

Bona told me that he systematically made himself do such an exercise. It's probably one of the reasons his work is so remarkable and seems like a challenge to the nihilism of the ambient artistic order. Heir to musical traditions that go from Francis Bebey and Manu Dibango to Milton Nascimento and Djavan, he does not use his heritage as a relic of the past whose survival he would try to celebrate, but to advance on new ground that he has conquered in the course of various discoveries and encounters—Jaco Pastorius of course, but also Harry Belafonte, Wayne Shorter, Joe Zawinul, Sadao Watanabe, Pat Metheny, Mike Stern, Herbie Hancock, Bobby McFerrin, Victor Wooten, and a few others. For him, tradition is simply a way to renew creation. And novelty is the instrument through which he reexplores his heritage. This kind of positioning permits him to change the functions of music: it is no longer content to offer a background for the merrymaking that is supposed to ward off the griefs of an often disastrous daily life, nor to celebrate the hazy heroism of this people that likes to reinvent its past, nor to accompany the upheavals of the social movement, nor even to produce a third-rate mysticism. It becomes once more an object of philosophical speculation and a locus of exploration of the soul's mysteries.

This approach to music, simultaneously cosmopolitan and antinihilistic, is evident in his musical aesthetics—notably the use of dissonance in his short compositions "Kivu" and "Muto Bye Bye." Still today, conservatives of classical theory postulate that a "good" musical phrase should end on a consonance. They consider dissonance a transitory element, a series of incomplete tonalities serving as punctuation. The technical role assigned to it is to arouse a feeling of expectancy in order to emphasize the resolving force of the consonance which alone perfects the construction by offering the ear a final chord all the more fitting in that it was anticipated. Bona has never considered himself a prisoner of the duty to satisfy those ticklish ears too used to the cozy comfort of academic compositions. Like some avant-gardists, he doesn't feel obligated to make a consonance follow a dissonance. For him, consonance and dissonance are individual entities freed from the functions prescribed for them by old music theory and usable independently of one another. Resolution is therefore neither a melodic obligation nor a harmonic imperative.

Several other African composers have attempted this same sort of change in paradigm, but less successfully. This was notably the case with Francis Bebey and Dollar Brand, who wanted to interest the general public in the "traditional" aspects of African music. Their assertions ran into a wall of silence and conventional critics rushed to categorize them as embittered people nostalgic for a long-gone past or a world that had never existed. Judged undecipherable, their compositions were more or less relegated to the shelf of folkloric caricatures in museums of African art created here and there in the West, either from pity or to make their founders feel good.

The innovations put forward by Bona differ from these preceding attempts: they involve a language that is denser and more daring, and a decided will to free himself from the spiritual anarchy and the agitated simplism which constitute the dominant framework of what is called "African music." His style thus distinguishes itself resolutely from the technical minimalism that all too often reduces this music to a repetitive, arid, and monotonous gesticulation. His music is punctuated by searing intensities and constantly traversed by the breath of the Universal. As a professor of harmony and improvisation at New York University, he can use to advantage the riches of various musical traditions—African American, Western, Latin-American, Indian—all the while giving a prominent place to the coherence and sobriety that give authenticity to his approach. He doesn't need the academic exuberance that enables some African artists steeped in Western musical theory to convince themselves that they too have become "important" composers. For cosmopolitanism reduced to sterile eclecticism or a simple play of virtuosities is ineffective. On the other hand, the quest of the universal, anchored in technical knowledge and the sensibilities of one's place of origin, seems to him to be the path of salvation and the means of freeing himself from the sickly nihilism of that dance music to which some people like to confine Africans.

# 4

## THE SAVOR OF SIN

### DIALOGUE AROUND GOD'S FUNERAL

God himself is not without sin, since he created the world.
—BULGARIAN PROVERB

My interviewer was not wearing a cassock. Relaxed, cocky, and with smiling pugnacity, this Catholic priest with the look of a playboy had been driven to my home by a courteous, silent woman whom he called his "daughter." Perhaps that was why I'd spoken to him openly about God, faith, religious ethics, sorcery, and many other subjects about which I'd always hesitated to express myself publicly. He was passing through Washington and had asked to interview me for the Cameroonian semimonthly periodical *L'Effort* of which he was the editor in chief. Not knowing him from Adam, I'd nevertheless spontaneously agreed to his request, thinking he'd been sent by Cardinal Christian Tumi, the archbishop of Douala who was one of my mentors during my time of political infamy.[1]

## Nervous Breakdown at the Vatican

We'd conversed for several hours. At some of my statements, he'd widened his mischievous little eyes and nervously tightened his grip on his tape recorder though without ever losing his affability. One can imagine my astonishment at learning a few weeks later that the interview had been rejected without explanation by the magazine, of which the priest was moreover no longer the editor in chief. He'd been "called to other duties," as they say over there.

The interview was probably not the reason for this inelegant, unexplained posting. But the priest was proud of having pried out of me what he considered confessions and did really want to publish them in the columns of the periodical from which he'd just been abruptly dismissed. Nothing doing: his successor at the magazine had declined the offer, not wishing to face the anger of his hierarchical superiors. Furious, the priest had immediately offered the interview to a local daily that had quickly featured it on the front page as a first-class journalistic scoop. Avid for anything sensational and speculative, Cameroonian readers had rushed to buy copies of the paper.

All this had further irritated a great many leaders of the Catholic Church of Cameroon. These cassocked proprietors of the Word of God had reacted by subjecting this decidedly heretical priest, as well as the editor in chief of the independent newspaper who had committed the crime of lèse-Vatican by publishing my remarks, to a mini-inquisition. And yet the two victims had taken the precaution of clearly distancing themselves from me by explaining in the introduction to the interview that my remarks did not reflect the ideas of the interviewer nor even of the paper that was publishing them! This weak subterfuge hadn't satisfied the Church leaders' thirst for vengeance, obsessed as they were with only one question: how could an experienced priest have taken part in what looked like an underhanded attempt to demolish the immutable truth of the Bible?

The archbishop of Douala, my mentor, had remained silent. The tempest was nonetheless taking place in the zone of his administrative and spiritual authority. As for the apostolic nuncio to Cameroon, though known as an eminent member of the local diplomatic community, he'd denounced in no uncertain terms the excessive tolerance with which he said I'd been treated. Having read in my remarks traces of deviltry that had made him lose his famed loquacity and good manners, he'd peremptorily summoned the poor priest to Yaoundé as soon as the interview was published, forcing him to travel several hundred miles on an awful road in the middle of the night. A very official request for explanations, coming directly from the Vatican, was inflicted upon the priest. Renouncing (provisionally?) the teachings of Christ, even forgetting that he'd spent years cultivating the image of a staunch defender of democracy and freedom of opinion, the nuncio also summoned the editor in chief of the newspaper in which the interview had appeared—a man who was convinced that his unshakable faith in God destined him for paradise—to express his anger. Speaking like Louis de Funès in Gérard Oury's *Le Corniaud (The Sucker)*, the Vatican ambassador shouted that it was "intolerable, intolerable!" that a paper for which he'd had until then a bit of respect would publish the heretical remarks on religion of a man obviously possessed by doubt. The Gospel was a unique, unshakable truth.

Those nocturnal meetings of the crisis committee held at the apostolic nunciature on the cold hills of Mont-Fébé in Yaoundé had been heated, as the Vatican diplomat remained angry at the "extreme gravity of the situation" and expressed his theories about the excesses of freedom of opinion. And yet the country had many other problems: clinging to power for a good half century, a government of visionaries had taken the future hostage. Every night, thousands of children with empty stomachs were sleeping on the shabby streets of this rich country. Millions of citizens were coping with suffering and helplessness by daily handing over their meager savings to witch doctors and charlatans.

All of that mattered little to the ambassador from the Vatican who was practically accusing me of having organized a public funeral for the Almighty God of the Catholic Church. He was interested in only one thing: restoring the dignity of the Church, extinguishing an invisible but as he saw it devastating fire that my remarks about religion and faith had ignited. He also had to calm his colleagues of the Holy See who, upon reading the interview, had nearly gone into hysterics. The only possible reparation consisted in publishing prominently in the paper a clarification restating firmly that the priest-interviewer did not share my diabolical opinions. This was done as quickly as possible. Despite the respect that the editor in chief of the paper felt for me, offending the representative of Pope Benedict XVI—a man surely endowed with mystical powers and capable of reserving a choice place in paradise or hell for heretical souls—was out of the question.

So it had taken nothing more than a little interview for the old relations I'd thought were at least cordial with certain dignitaries of the Cameroonian Catholic Church to suddenly totter and fray. A few words pronounced innocently about the mystery of faith and the uses of religion in Africa had thrown supposedly imperturbable and tolerant men into a turmoil. What had I said that was so serious that it almost merited excommunication? What impertinent remark had I made to justify such agitation?

### Hedonistic God or Incompetent God?

The conversation had begun with a clarification: my interlocutor wanted to know whether I believed in God. I could have provoked him by suggesting a nihilistic reading of faith and said like Emil Cioran that the invention of God comes above all from the human being's need for emptiness: "At a certain degree of solitude or intensity there are fewer and fewer people with whom one can converse; one finally even realizes that there isn't anyone like oneself. When one arrives at this extremity, one turns to those unlike oneself, to the angels, to God. So it is for lack of an interlocutor here below that one looks for another elsewhere . . . The only usefulness of God (or of the concept of God) is that he allows one to cut oneself off from men without falling into narcissism, delusions, disgust, all vicissitudes of the Self. One remains normal, with the illusion of an objective support. Additionally, believing in God exempts you from believing in anything else: which is an appreciable advantage."[2] I could have explained that faith for many Africans is a way of warding off disillusionment, of freeing themselves from the turpitudes of daily reality, of escaping the dictatorship of the self.

Yes, I believe in God, I answered, nevertheless explaining that my God was the one who reveals himself every day in the smiles of my children, or manifests himself in the heroic courage of simple, ordinary people who never let life's difficulties disturb their conscience or diminish their humanity. What's more, whether I believed didn't seem to me to be important for our conversation. "Oh yes, oh yes," the priest insisted, almost leaping from his chair. "It's extremely important because people have the impression that the more intellectual and bourgeois one becomes, the more one puts off indefinitely the notion of God . . ." As I had become neither intellectual nor bourgeois, I didn't feel that his sarcasm was aimed at me. I simply answered that faith is a personal matter. The debate about the existence of God seemed a bit ridiculous to me.

Ridiculous? The priest took off his glasses, cleaned them and put them back on before pleasantly ordering me to clarify what I meant. An endless, dead-end debate, I asserted. For even it if were proven that God does not exist, the idea of God would still be a fine invention of the human mind, as Dostoyevsky said. We shouldn't forget the positive externalities that faith can generate in each human being, just because God is often used by ethnocentrists around the world to ratify the existence of religious movements and corner the monopoly of spirituality and the treasures of the mind and even of reason, or because religious movements have often been vehicles of violent conflict. Besides, the four greatest destroyers of human life of the twentieth century—Hitler, Stalin, Mao, and Pol Pot—were militant unbelievers. Faith can be a source of moral elegance. One of my good Cameroonian friends, who never lets a day go by without saying his five prayers, constantly reminds me that prayer is above all an act of humility. Even if it simply serves to question our certainties, to confront doubt and thus to shoulder the obligation of modesty, its merit is not negligible.

As for the atheism at times noisily proclaimed by certain Africans, it doesn't bother me in the least. Besides the fact that I've always found an incompressible bit of spirituality—or religiosity—in Africans, even when they proclaim themselves to be atheists, I also believe that their indwelling quest for the Absolute and their desire for an ethics don't necessarily express themselves by belief in God. Atheists too are among the possible elect destined for paradise—if it exists. I'd come to this conclusion after a conversation with Cardinal Christian Tumi many years ago, at the time when, despite the international excitement about the meaning of the fall of the Berlin Wall, political repression was going strong in Cameroon. I was quite angry and had asked the cardinal why the just and merciful Almighty God let the Cameroonians suffer so much under the indifferent gaze of the international community. In my youthful hotheadedness, I'd even told him that God was either a bit sadistic and hedonistic, or totally overwhelmed by events and therefore surely not almighty...

The cardinal could have answered that God offered unhappiness to men so they'd have something to sing about, as Homer says in the eighth book of the *Odyssey*. He had simply smiled and answered that God was so tolerant toward me that he was leaving to each person the freedom to choose between good and evil, and to have an influence on his own destiny. And that he was also leaving me the freedom to judge him, and even to insult him... This little remark about God's extreme tolerance had disturbed me and made me feel guilty. It had inserted a bit of modesty into my approach to faith.

I'd then understood that it's very risky to have certainties—including for that matter the certainty of uncertainty. Turning a negation into a belief isn't necessarily great conceptual progress. But it's precisely the trap into which unbelievers fall easily: some antireligious movements are so obsessive that they become a form of religion. All do not unfortunately have the sense of humor of Jorge Luis Borges, who didn't believe in God, and said that religion is a branch of fantastic literature. For him, everything the great science fiction authors have written is nothing compared to the great myths of the Bible...

## Cost-Benefit Analysis of Faith

The conversation with the priest then moved to the political economy of faith and religion. "Do you go to church on Sundays?" he asked me with a highly suspicious air. He was looking at me as if he knew my answer in advance and dreaded it. I had to admit to him that that was an embarrassing question. I didn't go as often as I'd like. I couldn't take refuge behind the tiny excuse that I was a busy man. The fact of having a lot of work has never been a valid explanation for important things. The priorities one sets for oneself determine the order of values one chooses for oneself. And prayer supposedly legitimizes better than anything else the path of the believer. Martin Luther said: "I have so much business I cannot get on without spending three hours daily in prayer!"

The question made me understand that I was still a prisoner of narcissistic certainties that justified my unavailability for Church communion. In Douala, I'd stopped going to church. I didn't want to subject myself to the presence of the Republic's brigands in suits and ties who rushed to the front pews, sang off-key and louder than everyone else, as if to beg for the absolution of their many sins. And yet, when I asked Cardinal Christian Tumi why these notorious scoundrels could receive communion on Sundays, he suggested with his mocking smile that I mind my own sins and leave others to their consciences and to God.

No, I didn't go to church regularly. This semiconfession led the priest to ask me how economists approach

religion and what its social function was in today's
Africa. I reminded him that for Marxist economists, religion was the opiate of the people and therefore a simple
instrument used by capitalism for social hegemony. As
for the neoclassical economists who dominate the discipline today, they analyze the religious field as a simple
market. They see on one hand religious entrepreneurs and
on the other consumers who, consciously or unconsciously,
examine the benefits and costs of the various religions
and look for the best returns on their spiritual invest-
ments. This approach shocks many noneconomists, who
find it grotesque and mechanical for it neglects the value
of nonmarket transactions. Its basic postulate is, however, simple: human beings are rational agents who maximize their spiritual satisfaction and welfare by reacting
to incentive systems. Gary Becker was even awarded a
Nobel Prize for developing social theories following this
line of reasoning.

Traditional sociology claimed that the purpose of religion is to explain the sacred, that is, the unusual and
mysterious experiences of life, as opposed to the common
and banal, to everything that occurs repetitively in daily
life. This distinction is too schematic. In Cameroon, even
the most ordinary things quickly take a supernatural turn.
Simply crossing the street at the Ndokoti intersection in
Douala in the middle of the day, or finding potable water
coming from faucets is somewhat miraculous. As a result,
the common and the mysterious permanently overlap
in the daily life of Africans. It is therefore not surprising
that the sacred occupies a large space in our imaginary,

sustaining a need for spirituality that religion exploits to perpetuate itself.

Of course, religion seeks to answer existential questions about the goal of life, directions for its use and the choice of values. It helps many citizens confront existential doubt, reaffirm their identities and find a meaning for their lives. It strengthens social norms by giving them the status of divine laws. It also serves as an ethical vehicle for moral obligations like the duty of solidarity and compassion. It helps in confronting the great shocks of life and enables people to come to terms with the guilt that all Africans constantly feel faced with evil and suffering. But, despite these potential virtues, religion should be permanently subjected to a threefold critique: political, theological, and philosophical.

At these remarks, my interlocutor looked intrigued. He insisted that I clarify my thoughts. I didn't make much of an effort to reassure him. Politically speaking, the history of religion in Africa is certainly marked by courageous actions by atypical individuals. Still today, throughout the continent, a few churchmen are doing honorable work among populations, playing the role of social workers, mentors, confidantes, and even psychiatrists. But institutional religion in Africa also functions like the bureaucracies of the former one-party system. Many of its members ought to go to confession every day to expiate their sins and ask for absolution. Like the missionaries of the colonial period, they abusively use their positions of moral recourse to satisfy their fantasies of power. Others are paranoid and see evil everywhere. Prisoners of their bitterness and permanently at sea in microscopic tribal quarrels, they have a hard time with their vocations and constantly brood because they haven't been promoted to important posts. As if the fact of not being a bishop or cardinal gave them the impression of having been a failure in life. They recite the Bible every day and wear the cross of Jesus over their hearts, but are filled with enough anger and spite to make the least recommendable characters of the Bible shudder in amazement.

All in all then, I found the balance sheet of the African churches rather mixed, stained with colonial ambiguities and their incestuous relationships with oppressive political regimes. With regard to the Catholic Church of which my interlocutor was a representative, I recommended that it examine itself and confess its sins publicly. It needs to organize national conferences here and there to clarify its responsibility in some of the darkest episodes of African political history. "Every soul is hostage to its actions," says the Koran. It seemed to me that the metaphor of a public confession on the part of the Church would free it from the weight of the memory of its past actions and help diminish its lack of credibility. What better, indeed, than a mea culpa coming from the very mouths of the bishops, comparable to the forgiveness John Paul II had asked for to erase the guilty, complicit silence of Pius XI and Pius XII when faced with the fascism of Mussolini and Hitler?

The priest listened to me in silence, looking rather terrorized. I continued by explaining that, theologically speaking, what I don't like in monotheistic religions such as Christianity, Judaism, or Islam is that they claim to have the monopoly on virtue. To put things into perspective, I reminded him that several billion Chinese and Indians believe neither in Jesus Christ nor in Allah and that all those good people are surely not damned souls destined for hell. On the other hand, many priests and imams pray all day long, which doesn't prevent them from cheerfully committing the worst atrocities, sometimes even when coming from church or the mosque. Cassocks often hide all sorts of things, I'd said to him mischievously. Fortunately he wasn't wearing one that evening. He took the comment in silence and I took advantage of what seemed to be a brief moment of introspection on his part to add that polytheistic religions that proclaim the existence of several gods and even of a divine hierarchy are generally less sectarian. Ethical religions like Buddhism, Confucianism, Shintoism, or Taoism seem more modest, for they put less emphasis on the figure of a founding God and more on the principles one must respect to find internal harmony and social balance. As to older religions like African animism, they're having difficulty redefining themselves these days and seem to have fallen victim to the political and identity transformations of our time.

Philosophically speaking, certain fundamental postulates of Christianity don't seem very convincing. The myth of redemption, for instance, that makes naïve minds think that paradise is guaranteed them if they submit to a way of thinking, ought perhaps to be discussed. The priest had immediately stiffened in his chair: so redemption is only a myth? So Jesus did not die on the cross to save us? I felt in his questions the anxiety of a good Catholic priest seething with anger and I put his mind at ease so we could pursue a civilized dialogue. I like the idea and the problematics of Christ very much, I explained. I like the myths he embodies and the questioning to which he forces each of us in our daily life. I like the moral prescriptions toward which this idea urges us, and the illusion that we can all be perfect, like gods. For, since I'm not God, I put up with my imperfections and consider the ethical ideal set forth by Jesus as a horizon toward which we should try to direct ourselves. A bit like an asymptote in mathematics, a straight line approached by a curve which never really touches it and becomes one with it.

The priest continued to listen to me religiously. My judgment concerning the African churches as social institutions seemed to pose even more problems for him. I claimed that they tend to defend the existing cultural and social order. Faced with the great political, economic, and moral crises Africa is going through, the Conferences of Bishops merely publish indignant and moralizing communiqués from time to time to ease their consciences. When real action is necessary to refuse the unacceptable, combat evil, change things, engage in civil disobedience, go out into the streets to protect the citizens whose rights are being violated, most churchmen take refuge in their cassocks. They become invisible. They become mute. They just brandish the cross and say masses in Latin.

The mission of the Catholic Church is certainly not to put forward political systems or models of social organization, I admitted. The Vatican's Pontifical Council states this in its Compendium of the Social Doctrine of the Church. But the Code of Canon Law, which seems to me to be a superior legal source, states clearly that it is up to the Church to "proclaim moral principles, even in respect of the social order, and to make judgments about any human matter in so far as this is required by fundamental human rights or the salvation of souls." Based on this, I exhorted career-minded priests who plead fright of the Vatican gurus as an excuse for not acting to face up to their social responsibilities. I asked African religious leaders to stop playing at analyzing sacred texts and be bolder in citizen action. Instead of spending their time discussing the meanings of this or that Bible verse, the administrators of the revealed religions could do God's work on earth; that is, help people in a concrete way to better the condition of their lives. In a concrete way would mean, for instance, that they should firmly denounce African authoritarianisms or even simply be more vigorously engaged in solving problems of daily life, from road accidents that decimate populations and make people doubt the existence of God to the destruction of the ecosystem, which causes immense environmental damage throughout the continent. After all, people who promote the Bible or the Koran, which are full of incredible stories, cannot be devoid of imagination!

The priest retorted that I was reducing Christianity to its mere social welfare aspects at the risk of losing sight of its spiritual dimension. That was not what I meant. I simply thought that the African religious organizations have great potential power that could be used in service of social change. But this is underutilized because their hierarchy is dominated by conservative minds who prefer to take refuge in metaphysical discussions. I acknowledged that the Catholic Church has at times itself been a victim of the brutality of oppression. In Cameroon as elsewhere, some priests and sisters who took their mission of evangelization seriously have been murdered. The authoritarian governments have never published the results of investigations into these mysterious murders of members of religious orders. Unfortunately, the Vatican hasn't been very zealous in demanding justice. A silence heavy with meaning.

## Witch Doctoring and Sorcery

The conversation had taken on a more serious tone that I'd thought it would. My interviewer was now looking at me cautiously, as one looks at lost souls, beyond redemption. All the same, he had the decency to continue our dialogue, hoping that we'd talk about the spectacular development of the many religious cults that now clutter the African social landscape. He wanted to know what I thought of them. Perhaps we'd at least agree on the fact that this explosion of paganism was a dangerous development for African societies? There too, I had to disappoint him by pointing out that this type of phenomenon was not specifically African, and that all human civilizations are subject to its effects at some point or other in their history. Besides, this "proliferation of the divine" reflects above all the lack of credibility suffered by Christianity in Africa. Formulating the problem in economic terms, I told him that the success of the religious cults and paganism in the black world is the manifestation of a large deficit of spirituality on the official market, of a gap between the large ethical demand of the populations and the insufficient supply of spirituality from the traditional churches. Their dynamism reflects the emergence of a religious "black market." It is above all proof of the chronic incompetence of established churches, of their incapability to formulate appropriate social answers to the problems of our time and to offer a dream to populations often caught in the snare of destitution and inevitability. After all, "men follow only those who lavish illusions on them. You never see a crowd around a disenchanted person" (Cioran).

Some religious cults proclaim a more systematic opposition to the social order than the established religious institutions. This gives them strength and legitimacy in an environment marked by shortages and suffering. Their leaders are often eccentric gurus or decent fanatics who sometimes have good intentions but have gotten lost in their egos and don't always have a coherent intellectual and philosophical education. Moreover, they suffer from a Jesus syndrome and seriously believe they are the new Messiah. They establish themselves as neighborhood psychiatrists and offer comfort to troubled souls. Quite often, their religious cults propose "freer" and more audacious interpretations of the Holy Scriptures. In the context of the ethical poverty, collective suffering, and generalized depression found in many African countries, their voluntarist doctrines explain their success.

More audacious, other parareligious movements are directed to an audience that is well-educated but disoriented in the troubles of existence. The credulity of the faithful allows them to exploit the supernatural and encourage obscurantism in people despite their high level of education. In nations in a state of moral and economic bankruptcy, they create an atmosphere of confusion that serves the interests of political power: they give those who govern the leisure of offloading their responsibilities onto providence. Although they present themselves as organizations that question the order of things, in truth they uphold the status quo and the various prevailing forms of social nihilism. Their discourse is marked with theatricality: their prayers, for instance, are striking sessions of collective gesticulation, weeping, and purifying screams. But spiritually speaking, their "theology" does not differ fundamentally from that of the religious institutions from which they claim to distinguish themselves. It is, for that matter, not surprising that most African political leaders are often the most influential members of these parareligious movements whose chief function is to lull the vigilance and critical mind of the populace. This is notably true of Presidents Omar Bongo Ondimba of Gabon and Paul Biya of Cameroon.

These remarks relaxed my interviewer a bit. He pointed out to me that lumping together authentic African healers and village sorcerers was unjust, for the former have genuine knowledge whereas the latter simply exploit the naïveté of the people. Perhaps. Conceptually, one can imagine varying degrees of "seriousness" among the different actors occupying the field of religion and mysticism. In practice, it's impossible to establish a rigorous distinction among them. Some treatments offered by witch doctors and sorcerers fall into the category of so-called alternative medicine or intersect with biological psychiatry. Similar practices exist in the West, where alternative medicine uses syncretic methods like radionics, geobiology or radiesthesia (divination). Manic-depressive patients are sometimes treated with bold therapies including electric shocks or induced hypoglycemic comas. Well-established corporatist organizations of psychiatrists are in charge of overseeing the modes of validation of the scientific corpus and respect of professional deontology and a code of ethics. Furthermore, health ministries exercise at least an administrative supervision, which gives it legal responsibilities as well as the obligation of monitoring prescribed treatments.

I don't automatically doubt the merits of traditional African medicine of which sorcerers and witch doctors claim to hold the secrets. But when it takes place in a context characterized by absence of regulation and lack of an inventory of knowledge, separating the wheat from the chaff becomes practically impossible. Poverty, disappointed love, emotional trauma, an inability to manage the periods of depression that punctuate the ebb and flow of life, difficulties dealing with doubt: there are numerous factors that favor the emergence of charlatans claiming to know the "operating instructions" for life.

This veritable witch doctor boom is obvious in villages and cities alike, where zany individuals think they're endowed with therapeutic knowledge. These faith hucksters draw crowds in nocturnal processions and make of the misfortunes of others their stock in trade.

Most of these gurus are motivated by money; a few others by their own neuroses, their need to shine, or the desire to exact revenge for their own wretched lives. Autohypnosis and intoxication make them think they too have finally become "somebody." It's easy to understand them. They give a feeling of love and the illusion of being important to citizens of all social classes, to "big CEOs," ministers of the "Republic," or women of a social class to which they would otherwise not have had access. This new industry of depression is an effective life preserver for those in political power who support it by their silence, for it is also useful as an instrument of social control.

I reminded my interlocutor that an inflation of belief in occult powers and paranormal phenomena has moreover been observed in societies dealing with great economic difficulties. Between the thirteenth and nineteenth centuries, a good million people were executed in Europe for the crime of sorcery.[3] In the United States, outbursts of hysteria over devil possession led to the famous Salem witch trials in the seventeenth century. Belief in sorcery is a construct of the social imaginary that unfortunately has a cost. In Africa, it is stimulated by poverty, emotional deprivation, a lack of self-confidence, and fear. It is, incidentally, difficult to reconcile with faith in God: How can one trust an almighty and merciful Being while at the same time fearing the gesticulations of a lazy sorcerer walking around in the bush with bird feathers on his head and reciting abracadabras in the middle of the night?

A manifestation of this paradox: in a famous speech given in a city well-known for the aggressiveness and talent of its sorcerers, Cameroon's President Biya, a pious man who does not hesitate to proclaim his Christian faith publicly, called on his compatriots to combat sorcery. He reminded them that the Penal Code condemns sorcerers to prison terms that could be as long as ten years—forgetting that the state cannot reconfigure systems of belief and cosmogonies that are often very ancient by simply passing laws and issuing decrees. Unfortunately, as the law does not define what constitutes sorcery, the judges who regularly have to decide these affairs find themselves obliged to solicit the expertise of supposed sorcerers to identify other sorcerers! The courts are often the theater of hallucinations and magical practices for a good cause . . .

My interlocutor simply smiled. For him, African sorcery was a reality that couldn't be brushed away out of hand. It could not be reduced to a phenomenon linked to conditions of life and level of economic growth. "Despite their material affluence, some Westerners continue to believe in it," he pointed out. "Some of them even come to quench their thirst at the springs of African initiation rites! And many Cameroonians who've reached a certain level of social ease continue to believe in sorcery." I nonetheless continued my argument, trying to convince him by sketching a rapid sociological profile of the African nouveaux riches: many of them have gotten to an enviable social level not by the sweat of their brow, but by the luck of their schemes. So they're constantly haunted by the fear of falling back into destitution. They don't think they've permanently escaped poverty, since their brothers, cousins, aunts, uncles, nephews, and neighbors are still mired in it. As their fortunes and material possessions haven't been able to free their imaginary from the syndrome of destitution, they constantly need sorcerers to console themselves and ward off bad luck . . .

I explained that the way African educational systems are structured does not permit those who come out of them to free themselves from the arbitrariness of the beliefs in vogue. Whether, religious, private, or public, the schools and universities tend to produce administrative assistants, third-rate citizens. African managers and executives are thus often inferior products of the colonial education system, which hasn't changed though half a century has gone by since independence. That's why, on the psychological level, the social groups of African citizens are often much more alike than anthropologists will admit. Trapped by destitution, the poor choke with rage caused by injustice. The citizens who are well off wallow in futility and boredom and try to fill their lives by organizing orgies and parties where, in the words of Ivory Coast humorist Adama Dahico, they open champagne bottles using remote control devices. As for the intellectuals (or, more precisely, those with degrees), they've often been turned into jobless vagrants and many can be seen wandering the halls of the party in power like scrawny dogs waiting for someone to throw them a bone to gnaw . . .

Belief in sorcery in Africa must thus be seen against a philosophical background comparable to what Foucault called *episteme*—a set of relationships uniting different types of discourse within a given epoch. It's not a matter of a monolithic, unitary system of thought, coherent and closed in upon itself, nor an immutable historic constraint. Nor is it a matter of a great underlying theory of ways of seeing the world. The *episteme* that facilitates and legitimizes the collective belief in sorcery is rather "a simultaneous play of remanences," an articulation of multiple anchorage points, a bundle of abstract, arbitrary spiritual references that refer to one another and end up creating an overall network. It is nihilistic reasoning in that it constitutes a path pointing toward the nothingness of nonvalues and postulates self-doubt.

After these expositions, I stopped talking. The priest also assumed a taciturn air, without my being able to guess what he was thinking. My remarks had not seemed to reassure him as to the purity of my soul and the strength of my Christian faith. After several sighs heavy with meaning, he asked me once more about the initial subject; that is, the quality of my religious faith. It was getting late and I was no longer in the mood to avoid offending him. I admitted that my conception of spirituality was hard to reconcile with certain postulates of the Vatican's version of Christianity. The idea that a person receives in this life the punishments or rewards of a previous life didn't sit well with me. Not any better than the belief in the fatalism of certain mystics who claim that Africa's current difficult situation is the reflection of a sort of collective karma. I told him that this abdication of our humanity exonerates us from our immediate responsibilities and spares us the trouble of having to shape our becoming. Life is not a cosmic illusion.

In closing our discussion, the priest asked me if I thought myself worthy of paradise. No, I answered, I don't believe I merit either the laurels of paradise or the flames of hell. For that matter, this alternative seems to me to be one of the weaknesses of the Judeo-Christian philosophy. The idea of a God who threatens citizens with his wrath is not in keeping with his greatness. Worship of God should not be a result of fear of hell or hope of paradise. It should flow from an ethical demand peculiar to each believer. And I quoted the Persian poet Attar, who was a Sufi: "If I worship you for fear of hell, burn me in hell, and if I worship in hope of paradise, exclude me from paradise. But if I worship you for your own sake, do not grudge me your everlasting beauty" *(The Conference of the Birds)*.

# 5

---

# ETHIC OF THE USES
# OF THE BODY

## A THEORY OF SELF-ESTEEM

How does it feel to be a problem?

—W. E. B. DU BOIS, *The Souls of Black Folk*

When people do not respect us we are sharply offended;
yet in his private heart no man much respects himself.

—MARK TWAIN

**H**arry Belafonte, an artist and activist in progressive
African American causes, tells of painful childhood
memories about his mother Millie. Not those concerning
the material poverty or racism suffered by the family of
Caribbean emigrants in the United States in the 1930s
and 1940s. Rather, things all the more painful because
they are ordinary, insignificant. Millie was a Jamaican
immigrant who'd arrived in New York with no formal
education. Her husband, a native of Martinique who was
a cook in the British navy, was often away. Solitude, poverty, and illiteracy had changed neither the sense of duty

of this good mother, nor the ambitions she had for her children. To raise them, she had to exploit her only possession—her body. She had to present it well and keep it up well. Winter and summer, she'd put on her best clothes and join hundreds of other black women who lined up on Park Avenue to wait for hours for the improbable chance of earning a bit of money as housemaids. On some days an American woman would deign to inspect them and choose several of them who were then lucky to work for a few hours or a weekend as cleaning women at her home. But the wait was often in vain.

Millie knew how to maximize her physical capital. By dint of treating her body well, she looked neat enough to be able to clean the homes of the city's important wealthy families. This is how she'd managed to get a job as a maid, which gave her the revenue to offer her children dreams. When she came home from work, she'd tell her children about her experiences. She'd also bring newspapers that she tried hard to decipher to give them an idea of the events of the world in which they lived. Her manual labor had enabled her to offer her children, if not an education, at least a certain order of values and a reading of life, a way of interpreting the sounds of the world.

Emil Cioran despised his mother, who had told him after reading his first book that, if she had known in advance what kind of man he'd become, she would have had an abortion. He didn't begin to feel respect for her until the day when, to his very great surprise, she said to him: "For me, there's only Bach." To learn like this that she too could feel the ecstasy and miracle that only music creates enabled him to rediscover her. Unlike Cioran, Belafonte never despised his mother. Perhaps because of his musician's soul that permitted him to apprehend instinctively this unspeakable privacy in each individual revealed by the love of music. Had she been a prostitute, he would have admired her all the same, unreservedly. For Millie was one of those black women for whom manual labor and the use of the body implied no shameful act; they were, on the contrary, sovereign manifestations of the refusal of failure and illusion, the sign of what Cioran described as a "desperate and dangerous case of lucidity."

Nonetheless I've sometimes wondered what effect such memories had on Harry Belafonte's learning about life. What kind of scar does such humiliation leave on a child's innocent soul? What could it have meant to his imaginary to see his mother use her body—not in shameful acts, it should be added—as an instrument of survival in this America that was long the headquarters of slavery? And how did Millie herself accept the obligation of doing manual labor as the only means to live at a subsistence level?

His story brings us back to the tremendous amount of nihilism that has always marked the different ways of approaching the body in sub-Saharan African societies—and beyond. Representations of the body do not seem to have changed much in the course of the ages. Millions of women continue to act today as they did yesterday, cultivating a certain image of their bodies, devoting to them a maintenance budget that gives them a chance of pleasing, seducing, or living. Management of the body has even become an art of survival and an obsession. New markets (supply and demand) have developed, stimulated by the general increase in life expectancy, medical and technological advances, globalization, and the proliferation of virtual exchange sites. In these complex dynamics, researchers in the social sciences tend to focus on the sensationalism of current events. Reflection on the body is thus dominated by ethical discussions around the illicit trade in human organs or biological manipulation, so-called cultural practices like excision, traffic in humans, the exploitation of children for mercenary or military ends, and so forth. Or, quite often, media hype on these questions simply reflects the occasional need of the international community to ease its conscience.

Harry Belafonte's childhood memories invite us to revisit the philosophical ambiguities of the body, this privileged locus where the "being-in-itself" *(en-soi)* and the "being-for-itself" *(pour-soi)* of each person is expressed (Maurice Merleau-Ponty). Through the ages and civilizations, the body has always had a normative function and has reflected social patterns, the production of strategies of survival, and modes of organizing reality. In sub-Saharan African communities, its role in the production of discourse on oneself and others is increasingly important. Like Millie, many African men and women subvert the moral and philosophical theories traditionally assigned to trade in human bodies. They attribute to their bodies nobler functions, transforming them into vehicles of self-reappropriation, even in the worst of circumstances.

They use their bodies to reaffirm their dignity, thus establishing them as instruments of a nihilistic view of existence.

## The Thinking Body

Every human society secretes a minimal amount of bad taste that it needs to establish its norms, ratify its arbitrary aspects, and maintain its wish for a clear conscience. The collective desire for the morbid, for example, that leads people to gather spontaneously around a street fight or a traffic accident, is an essential ingredient of life in common. The need for bad taste has often expressed itself with tranquil cruelty. This was the case during several centuries, when slavery and the slave trade were not only ordinary forms of commerce, but also the foundation stone of social and economic development in the countries proclaiming themselves to be morally and philosophically the most advanced. All one need do to convince oneself is to look at some of the items advertising the sale of slaves in the eighteenth-century United States. One of them, appearing in the *New York Journal* of June 23, 1768, shows four black silhouettes under the large headline: "Negroes for Sale." With the serene assurance expected at the beginning of a marketing campaign for the sale of farm animals or agricultural implements, the text states that these slaves—among them girls of twelve and sixteen—were capable of hard work, and were therefore "recommendable."

Slavery as an operation of public sale and purchase of the bodies of Negroes was officially abolished in the state of New York, the epicenter of this flourishing commerce, in 1827, fifty-one years after the proclamation of American independence. This ban was not integrated into the federal Constitution until the ratification of the Thirteenth Amendment in 1865, at the end of the Civil War. For more than half a century after the mythical Founding Fathers (themselves slave owners) of virtuous America had feverishly proclaimed their great ambitions of moral and political reform in the Declaration of Independence, market forces thus peacefully continued to manage the bodies of these men, women, and children, whose status as human beings was questioned.

Slavery was, however, much more than a business. It was a debate about the body—that is, about the ambiguous and at times conflicting relationships that the human being has with himself, others, and good and evil. Through the ages and civilizations, the body has successively incarnated the image of the divinity, of life, but also of the demon and death. Perception of it has changed a great deal, going from the simplistic dualism (body-soul) of the Greeks and Romans to the biological determinism inspired by philosophical concepts derived from Darwinism. If the United States paid a heavy tribute to impose upon itself the official abolition of slavery (at least six hundred thousand dead during the Civil War, the assassination of Abraham Lincoln, and social rifts that are still deep today), it is because the southern states, where black slave labor was indispensable to maintain the profitability of cotton plantations, did not accept the imposition of a new morality from the North. The body was not perceived only as raw material. As the locus of validation of the power one possessed over others, it was also the space where self-awareness was expressed. It was thus a locus of production of discourse.

The body has not always been taken as seriously in the West. For a long time, it was only a simple carnal envelope containing biological machinery. Philosophers preferred the soul or spirit, the temple of thought and action, where the essential breath of life was thought to dwell. The body was then only a more or less shameful mass, destined in any case, to become ugly and weak and to destroy itself as it aged. Immaterial and invisible, the human spirit was celebrated as the most beautiful and important thing. Condemned to death, Socrates was happy about his sentence, claiming that he who had lived as a philosopher should see in death the supreme good that permits the separation of body and soul and gives the latter the opportunity to truly blossom.

This depreciation of the body is also to be found in Plato, who reduced it to the state of the tomb of the soul, and in Descartes, for whom the body was only an assembly of organs and members. His experience of the *cogito* ("I think therefore I am") was the logical outcome of an intellectual approach radically separating the biological from the psychical.[1] Aristotle had been more balanced on the question of body-soul dualism, defending the idea of an indestructible linkage between those two notions whose interaction constituted for him the human being in its integrity. "[The soul] is not a body, but something which belongs to a body," he writes in his *Treatise on the Soul*.

Theories and representations of the body in sub-Saharan African communities tend to reject the body-soul/spirit opposition, postulating rather a total osmosis of the various components of the human being, who is moreover considered as an integral part of a broader social body. Thus the idea of a cosmic physiology is celebrated, in which each body is only a fraction of a visible and invisible whole. Going beyond the body-soul dualism, such an approach does not view individuals without the society to which they belong. That is why Kenyan philosopher John Samuel Mbiti says ironically about Descartes's *cogito ergo sum:* "I am because we are; and since we are, therefore, I am." The body of an individual is thus only a link in a chain that must be seen as a whole if one wants to get an exact idea of it. Focusing only on the analysis of a body while ignoring its social connections amounts to looking at the wrong object, lacking perspective, and practicing a sociology of appearances.

The soul is therefore considered an integral part of the body, as is the spirit. All spirituality and all knowledge are physical elements of what one is. The Bambaras, for instance, proclaim: *"Maa ka Maaya ka ca a yèrè kònò."* Literal translation: "The people of the person are multiple in the person." Fulani and Bambara traditions, for that matter, consider that the human being is a sort of complex recipient, which "implies an internal multiplicity, concentric or superimposed planes of existence (physical, psychological and spiritual at various levels), as well as a constant dynamism" (Amadou Hampâté Bâ). The human person is thus never reduced either to the body, or to a monolithic entity. It is a permanent dynamism of which the body is both the reflection and the symbol.

This philosophy of the body has not, however, prevented the emergence of a biological determinism that has served, in the course of the years, to justify the construction of difference. As in many other societies, bodily morphologies have thus served to validate social categorizations, create hierarchies of ethnic groups, sanctify lines of power sharing, legitimize dynastic approaches, and justify sexual domination and exclusions. The body-producer of discourse is also a locus of expression of prejudices. Skin color, and the shape of eyes, the mouth, or the nose have become ways of categorizing the soul. We are here not far from the genetic reductionism of a certain Darwinian sociobiology that considers the body as the principal indicator not only of an individual's destiny, but also of his social itinerary. Did Nietzsche share this vision, he who considered the body as the essential vehicle of the human condition, like a powerful master of which the mind is only the instrument?

Millie, Harry Belafonte's mother, didn't have to read *Thus Spoke Zarathustra* to consider her body as an interface with the world, as a medium through which she wanted to define her relation to the world. Her body was the locus of expression of her family responsibilities and her social ambitions, the depository of her dreams of greatness, the privileged space of staging appearance and of the subtle play of seduction, and the anchorage point of the self. She constantly cared for its image in order to break free from the humiliations of slavery and memory.

## The Suffering Body

The body has at times been an instrument of political and economic management and regulation. In most ancient civilizations, among others those of Mesopotamia, India, and China, slavery was an activity essential to political stabilization and economic prosperity. It was also a mode of distributing power and a way of ratifying the order of values. Slaves were used for domestic tasks in homes and businesses or for extensive work in construction and agriculture. They constituted the labor force of the Hebrews. The Egyptians used them to build their royal palaces and monuments to the glory of the pharaohs. In the pre-Columbian civilizations of America (Aztecs, Incas, or Mayas), they were used chiefly as soldiers.

In the United States, the weight of racial fantasies associated with Negroes' genitals further complicated the relations between master and slave. The economic rationality put forward to justify the slavery of blacks sometimes hid unspoken racial and sexual convictions that were at least an equivalent motivation. Castration of male slaves and rape of the women put the finishing touches to social control, stripping the Negroes of the minimum of self-respect they still had. The body of the slave was the locus where not only the master's property rights, but also the slave's duty of submission in accepting his social condition, materialized.

Even when he was set free, the slave had to accept having inscribed onto his body a mark that forever distinguished him from his former master. In Rome, for example, there was a slave market where owners, filled with remorse and wishing to cleanse their consciences, would go to free their subjects. After a mock trial held on the Forum near the temple of Castor and Pollux, the slave would prostrate himself one last time before a magistrate to receive a symbolic lash. He would then rise, free, having become a Roman citizen. Nonetheless, he remained tied to his former master, whose name he took on. This obligation, moreover, extended to his offspring. His body had to suffer to serve as his symbolic passport to freedom.

The destruction of an enemy's body was long the ultimate ritual of supreme power. It wasn't enough to put an end to the lives of those considered implacable adversaries; their bodies had to be broken up and stripped of all dignity, even after their lives had been taken. Georges Balandier tells, for instance, of the cruelty with which a team of French resistance fighters he belonged to during the Second World War had treated German prisoners who'd attempted to escape: "Deliberations didn't take long; the decision was predictable: the three prisoners known to be guilty and still a threat were condemned to death. Volunteers made up an execution squad . . . Each condemned man was given a shovel so he could dig his grave . . . The others, lined up, would witness the unbearable ceremony . . . Orders, a single salvo, the bodies crumpled as though disarticulated; the sergeant finished them off with a shot in the head . . . The bodies were covered with rocks, earth, and branches by two of the prisoners. No material sign would permit them to be found, nothing but erasable traces."[2]

Humiliation of the adversary's body for political ends can go as far as the desecration of a corpse. The treatment given by the French colonial administration to the corpse of Ruben Um Nyobe, the leader of Cameroon's independence movement, illustrates this strategy. After his assassination in a village in the south of the country on September 13, 1958, his body became the property of the state. The populace was invited to come and look at it, to see for themselves the failure of the one whom legend had declared invincible and even the holder of a magic potion making him invulnerable to bullets. A government tract featuring a photo of Um Nyobe's corpse and jeering at "the God who'd been wrong" was immediately circulated throughout the country. His corpse was dragged through the mud from the place where he'd been killed to the village of Liyong where the peasants who'd known him well were forced to identify him. This triumphal march of the colonial army disfigured and tore his body to pieces. He was made to lose his human aspect in order to present to the people who had admired him a man without skin, without a head, and without a face.

The corpse was put on display in a dispensary. The head of a local militia financed by the colonial administration publicly heaped insults on it while striking the forehead. He even urged the corpse to get up and pit itself against him in a duel, so that the population of the village could see for itself which of the two was the stronger ... The body was then immersed in a massive block of concrete buried in the earth. "The state thus sought to permanently sever Um's ties with the soil in which he lay, and where, according to the indigenous principle of the society from which he descended, his relationship with his lineage and his descendants was perpetuated. It was a matter, in sum, of erasing Um from the memory of men by sending him to the chaos where he would very definitely no longer be anyone."[3] The physical assassination of the political adversary is thus not sufficient: the symbolical crushing of the corpse is also necessary to humiliate his memory and destroy his myth—and show the strength of the colonial power to the populations that sympathize with the independence movement.

This metaphoric assassination of Um Nyobe's corpse marked a new stage in the principle of humiliating the body of a political adversary in the African context. In comparison, the simple hanging of nationalist leaders Rudolf Douala Manga Bell and Martin-Paul Samba by German colonists in 1914 seems almost an aesthetic act, a surreptitious homage to their bodies, which did not deserve to be violated. After independence, President Ahmadou Ahidjo, a pure product of the colonial power of which he was nothing but the new face, made do with having his political adversaries shot in public—not without taking care to invite the population to come in crowds to see the spectacle. Secret police officials then made arrangements to discreetly find a shabby burial place for the famous corpses and get rid of those less well-known in common graves.

Other African autocrats like Zairian Mobutu Sese Seko were more eccentric in their treatment of their political adversaries' corpses. According to Dominique Sakombi Inongo, one of his ex-ministers, Mobutu believed in magic and charms, and slaked his thirst for power by drinking glasses of the blood of his victims . . . Like the Roman emperor Caligula, he enjoyed humiliating his ministers by having sexual relations with their wives. In the documentary film *Mobutu, roi du Zaïre,* Sakombi Inongo states that he himself had offered his wife to Mobutu, whose violence he feared. Quite a nihilist concept of conjugal love to offer the charms of one's own wife to conciliate humiliation and instinct for survival!

## The Body Rehabilitated

The body has not always been the symbolic locus where fear of self and scorn of others are expressed. It has at times served as an agency validating the most secret desires and accepting the inevitability of things. Then grounds for pride are found for it, or an attempt is made to endow it with qualities that make of it an indispensable aid in enduring the fatigue of time or outwitting the vigilance of death and aging, which is merely its agent. That is why, since the *Iliad* and the *Odyssey,* literatures the world over describe and magnify a certain aesthetic of the body, which helps people delude themselves and psychologically delay the fatal end. Writers and artists celebrate epic heroes whose larger-than-life bodies incarnate the community's values and ambitions. The canons of this aesthetic vary from one society to another, but the qualities extolled (strength, courage, sense of honor and duty, and so forth) are often similar. The cult of the body has even become somewhat excessive, particularly when advertising uses it to sell all sorts of products.

The black body has also benefitted from this rehabilitation: it is no longer only a locus of sadism and masochism, of humiliation and oppression. It is even presented as an asset, an attribute of dignity. The novel *Things Fall Apart* by Nigerian writer Chinua Achebe speaks, for example, of the beautiful wrestling-champion body of protagonist Obi Okonkwo, at times in a way reminiscent of the martial qualities of Homer's characters. In the West, a black body occasionally even represents currently fashionable exotic conceptions of beauty. Josephine Baker and Naomi Campbell are examples of this. In the same way, Mohamed Ali's and Michael Jordan's fine athletic bodies have emerged in advertising, beside those of other athletes with blond hair and blue eyes.

Postcards and coffee-table books on Africa are now illustrated with beautiful black bodies that appeal to a certain Western fondness for exoticism. They thus feature Fulani shepherds with hieratic bearing, Tuareg riders in ocher ponchos, or slim Masai warriors in form-fitting red loincloths. These images that kindle the fantasies of many tourists illustrate a new, almost cosmic, dimension of the black body. The exaltation of this body's beauty should not, however, make one forget the cohort of prejudices it conveys about black sexuality, which remains a source of bigotry, fear, and the rationalization of hierarchies between the races.

The social image of femininity has also evolved. For a long time, the ideal of beauty in Africa was the silhouette of the noble, graceful, lady with slim hips and pointed breasts. In New York as in Abidjan, people fantasized looking at photos of Marilyn Monroe, and pictures of her decorated students' dorm rooms. The success of this type of feminine silhouette was not due only to the uniformizing power of international fashion. It is also explained by the fact that the collective gaze becomes accustomed to the symmetry of forms, to quantitative norms of harmony, and to a certain conception of the aesthetic. Things change. New conceptions of the body's beauty are being validated. The ideal of the pretty woman, inevitably tall and slender like the models on the glossy pages of fashion magazines, is no longer current in many regions of Africa. The most highly prized beauty contests celebrate women who would formerly have been classified as rather "ugly." One of the most famous is the election of the "most beautiful fat woman" of Burkina Faso (Miss Poogbeêdre), the object of which is to "crown the beauty of well-endowed girls." During this annual event, corpulent women do indeed have the place of honor . . .

The ideal of youth and slimness that leads many women in the West to throng to gyms and pay close attention to their diets is silently combated in some societies, where the body is dressed simply and calmly accepts aging and settling into a routine. Watching a dressed body moving serenely in Senegal, Catherine Ndiaye writes: "The sagging of the fleshy, worn body becomes a sort of lasciviousness beneath the fabric. A form that moves and that is beautiful in its slow, irregular movement. The roll of flesh of its hips is a continuation of the gait, swaying above each step and softening it. The flabbiness of the re-laxed flesh is entirely converted to sensuality, dissipating in languor and forming a sort of attractive aura around a slightly stiffened corpulence; the stomach of the well-fed produces a sort of ampleness that at the same time cre-ates a reified image of security."[4] Old age is perceived nei-ther as a curse nor as a sign of social incompetence. An aged body is, on the contrary, a mark of wisdom, as well as the symbol of a full life, worthy of respect. "The "old man" cannot be checked off as a rundown being; he cannot be considered ugly due to his age, since his bodily wear is the written and directly legible trace of the life he knows through and through. Seen in this way, the parch-ment of the skin becomes a whole of captivating, impres-sive signs."[5]

African conceptions of the female body have evolved along with social, economic, political, and religious dy-namics. Locus of reproduction and thus of the perpetua-tion of the species, the female body is also the conflictual space where contradictory feelings exist side by side—dangerous appetites and human weaknesses—and where desire and distrust are expressed. It is always "a place of contestation and affirmation," a terrain "where different discourses on social practices, beliefs, and free will meet"

(Nathalie Etoke). It remains a sort of social thermometer enabling one to capture the current climate and the vision society has of itself. It is therefore an object of particular attention. The physical hygiene to which women must submit, appearance, wardrobe, and the rituals of stylishness continue to promote an idea of physical perfection reflecting a high degree of ethical demand. But the canons of beauty in vogue even in rural areas are no longer defined by the New York or Parisian fashion exchange. They are negotiated day to day according to the order of values of each epoch—that is, according to changing social dynamics.

## Tyrannical Beauty

Millie had understood: the defense of the body and the cult of beauty are also linked to social and economic demands. It is admittedly difficult to define rigorously what this beauty means, for each society sets its own criteria and adjusts to its own arbitrary aspects. The subjectivity of the criteria of beauty does not make them any less relevant: various studies using rigorous statistical techniques show, for instance, that there is a premium on the body's beauty on the job market in almost all societies. In China, the results of surveys and econometric analyses show that women's spending on beauty products and services not only improves the perception the public has of them, but also their earning level. Everywhere in Europe, studies by researchers in the social sciences have reached similar conclusions. Even the American Economic

Association, whose members had doubts about the economic and social power of the body's beauty, was quite embarrassed when an econometric study conducted by Daniel S. Hamermesh proved that the candidates with the best chances of being elected as directors were those whom the voters considered the most handsome...[6] Those poor researchers should have read Harry Belafonte's memories about his mother: beauty has become a diploma, a supplementary qualification needed to improve one's chances of success on the job market.

Given that one does not necessarily choose the bodily image one projects to others, such a state of affairs nonetheless poses the problem of the arbitrariness and injustice. It even creates new forms of discrimination against people who don't have a "pretty" face or a "nice" body. In the United States, a growing judicial corpus now forbids all discrimination on the job market based on physical appearance—which is an implicit way to negatively define the ideal of beauty: the law thus posits that any person who is intellectually qualified is assumed to be "pretty" enough to hold just about any job. Laws penalize employers guilty of discriminating against their employees on the basis of height, weight, or age. A decision by the Vermont Supreme Court sets precedent. It stipulates: the fact that a chambermaid has no teeth cannot be held against her by an employer because it constitutes a "handicap" protected by the law of this state (Fair Employment Practices Act)...[7]

Millie also understood that, beyond its utilitarian function dictated by market demands, the body has also become an instrument of self-valorization. As such, it necessitates particular attention, even constant "face-lifts" and "improvements." The treatment given it is a mode of social positioning and at times serves as a visa to pass from one social class to another. This explains the development of practices like tattoos, piercings, and many other modes of rehabilitating the body, which are no longer only cultural practices or fashion trends, but represent ways of asserting one's right to beauty.

In Cameroon, the common man often speaks with admiration of the "folded necks" to designate those wealthy people who wear like a badge of honor the wrinkles that the good life has supposedly printed on the napes of their necks. In Congo, they celebrate the "administrative belly" dragged about and cultivated by some senior officials to whom portliness gives bearing and self-confidence. Throughout sub-Saharan Africa, people straighten their hair (or dye black, frizzy hair blond) and use cosmetic products to lighten their skins, either because they are convinced of the seduction potential of an artificially lightened body (even if yellowish), or because show-business stars, like singer Koffi Olomidé, do it. It's their way of taking seriously what Eleanor Roosevelt liked to say: "No one can make you feel inferior without your consent."

This frenetic glorification of the body can be seen throughout the world. Asia is the principal center of the world market for pharmaceutical skin-lightening products. In Japan, more than a quarter of the personal care products contain active ingredients for skin lightening. The sums that the country devotes to them every year are greater than the annual budget of Burkina Faso . . . The North American market, focused on lightening age spots, is also not negligible. In China, more and more middle- and lower-class young women are having their eyes artificially "un-slanted." Jean-François Mattéi gives a good summary of the situation: "Body image has thus become a major narcissistic and professional issue where desire rivals frustration at being only what one is. From the anxiety about his 'look' that torments the adolescent to the worry of the mature man with graying temples who fears the disgrace of wrinkles or the degeneration of baldness, one cannot help thinking that our society conveys a materialistic vision of the person."[8] The body's beauty has practically become an insidious form of dictatorship to which increasingly broad segments of populations voluntarily submit for it is a manifestation of self-awareness.

## Undisguised Slavery

To measure the significance of these treatments of the human body and what they reveal about the techniques of the self, one must go beyond the mere wish to please, and ponder the other underlying motivations. Granted, a large proportion of organ donations are due to altruistic considerations by those who wish to help others, either while they are living or after their death. Kidneys are thus shared by members of the same family. Blood banks daily save thousands of lives throughout the world, benefitting from the generosity of anonymous benefactors who offer part of themselves to improve the conditions of life of others. But the spectacular development of body markets also reveals the propensity of a growing number of people to use their physical bodies as a source of revenue. This then is no longer simply a matter of aesthetic self-valorization or valorization of an ethic of altruism, but of financial self-valorization.

For the people behind this new trade that some liken to a new form of slavery, the body is merely a piece of merchandise like any other, a product likely to generate profit. Whether or not it is connected to a soul is unimportant, for it is seen as a collection of organs, and so as an ordinary commodity. The basic tools of microeconomics can be used to examine the structure and functioning of the global market of body parts. Supply, demand, quantity, shortage, and surplus thus help explain the price levels. Increase in life expectancy brings with it a constant increase in the global demand for human organs, and the development of financial markets, of the Internet, and progress in surgery facilitate exchanges and trafficking. Methods of valuating and assessing human existence have been developed by financial experts and are used in various branches of law like insurance law. This makes the moral acceptance of a body market commonplace.

Ethical norms regarding the treatment of the body are moreover changing rapidly: in the name of the great principles of respect of the human person and bodily integrity, the sale of organs is officially forbidden in many countries. On the other hand, the free gift of body components or their donation to medicine for scientific or therapeutic use is generally authorized and encouraged.

It is obvious however that the large imbalance between supply and demand creates shortages almost everywhere, favoring the emergence of an international black market where prices are determined according to principles of rarity, potential earnings, commissions charged by intermediaries, and the evaluation of the risk run by sellers and buyers.

The official abolition of slavery has thus not put an end to the question of the *commodification* of the human body. Throughout the world, trade in humans continues, at times taking underground forms or posing as supposed cultural practices like those of castes. This is aggravated by the extravagance of an extreme conception of capitalism that seems to have democratized the probability of being a victim of exploitation of the body: implacable market practices and deregulation of capital flow, which every country must imperatively attract in great quantities to finance investment and the creation of jobs, favor the emergence of illicit activities. Everything that can stimulate an increase in the gross domestic product (GDP) is stealthily encouraged. John Kenneth Galbraith ironically discussed the method of calculating GDP, the sum of value added shown by a country's companies and chief indicator of national economic health. He noted humorously that revenue coming from prostitution is included, whereas "pure" lovemaking that stimulates the life of a couple has no market value and is not measured as contributing to national wealth and the GDP...

On the part of the victims, several attitudes can be distinguished: first, those of people who find themselves enmeshed against their will in mafia networks and are the object of body trafficking. They naturally dream of attaining if not a semblance of human dignity, at least the feeling of freedom. Investigations of international prostitution networks show that the trauma of loss of liberty often permanently scars the soul. Their habituation to humiliation and their high degree of tolerance of pain and distress bring to mind the comment by Sacha Guitry: "I never feel truly free unless I'm locked in. When I turn the key, I'm not locked up; I'm shutting away the others."

Then there are the consenting victims, whose motives often vary: does a person who can't come to terms with obesity and resorts to aesthetic surgery to boost their self-esteem, to be more readily accepted by society, or to have a better chance of finding a job have the same ethical concerns as a person who feels obliged to sell a kidney to escape famine? Can one establish a moral equivalence between poor farmers in northern Burkina Faso who are forced by poverty to sell the work—that is, the bodies—of their children, and those African women who emigrate from Dakar, Lagos, or Douala to New York and Zurich to practice high-class prostitution?

These victims deliberately enter the new body markets with the nihilism of people who don't believe in happiness and don't burden their minds with metaphysical concerns. Prostitution and other trades of the body are, to them, occupations like any other. They consider that any investigation that goes too deeply into professional ethics or the "quality" of each human being's existence is unhealthy and demoralizing. Life is bearable

only because one doesn't think too much about individual destinies, because one doesn't get totally involved
in one's thoughts. To have the slightest chance of success,
any career choice must moreover include a certain dose of
illusion. For total lucidity means the end of all will, guaranteed discouragement, nothingness. Besides, the body
is not only what one is, but also what one has. It is a financial asset, an instrument of production, a means of
subsistence. As for freedom, in the final analysis it is only
a mirage hemmed in by laws, regulations, and social
norms, which is in reality "the faculty of choosing one's
own limits" (Jean-Louis Barrault).

The true novelty of the body market is thus neither the
frenzy with which people seek organs in a context of
shortage, nor even the cynicism of the traffickers, but the
need to survive and control their own humanity of those
who believe they must sell their organs so as not to die of
hunger, or even because of cupidity. Human organs (particularly kidneys) thus become financial assets or forms
of saving that are cheerfully converted into cash. A few
years ago, the online auction site eBay had to stop the
public sale of a human kidney. The advertisement posted
by someone living in Florida was soberly, yet temptingly,
worded: "Functioning human kidney for sale. You can
choose either of the two. The buyer will have to pay all
medical and transplant costs. Obviously, only one kidney
is for sale since I need the other to survive. Serious offers
only." At the time bidding was halted, bids for the kidney
had reached the sum of 5.7 million dollars ... A few
months later, a baby was offered at auction on the same

site, to "democratize" the access of sterile couples to the joys of paternity and maternity.

Moralistic proclamations about the inviolability of the body are not enough to prevent the use of the body for mercenary ends, the rental and loan of a uterus, or the marketing of babies. This physical or mental dismantling of the organism with respect to the body, and of the body with respect to the person, raises the question of "the existence of a subjective right to do what one likes with the components or functions of the body, or inversely to appropriate the body of another" (Catherine Labrusse-Riou). The consent of the supposed victims of such trafficking weakens the stigmatization of such new uses of the body. One must now ask why millions of people throughout the world are increasingly deliberately supplying mafia economic networks with their physical privacy and their organs.

How have we come from the age when slavery was an economic activity determined by power relationships and brutally imposed on those who were its victims, to a world where more and more people are deliberately selling their bodies to the highest bidder? How has the trade in bodies that caused a civil war in the United States and gave rise to new moral norms in the West become a branch of industry and a source of profit like others? How has the moral heritage of habeas corpus that determined Western thought and attitudes regarding human rights for many centuries been subverted to the point of today being interpreted as the right to freely sell one's kidney or any other organ of one's body?

Here again, Millie's choices offer food for thought: the body is not only the reflection of a static self-awareness. It is also the vehicle of the ambitions one harbors. Its exploitation is considered as an intellectual (and almost moral) obligation necessary to survival. Despite its increasing commercialization in the course of the centuries, it remains a powerful producer of discourse. Discourse about oneself at the same time as discourse about the other, since it is the locus where the poor and destitute call out to what remains of humanity's collective consciousness. For the poor, it allows them to have great ambitions for themselves and to write (if only tentatively) the trace of a life in a broader and more "respectable" narrative mode. It allows them to dream of other possibilities, and to position themselves outside of prejudices. It allows them to gradually eliminate lack of self-esteem and dignity. This manner of reinventing the techniques of the self reveals a mode of existence and a status of the philosophical subject that is no longer a procedure determined a priori but rather a reality freely elaborated according to specific forms of subjectivity. Emmanuel Kant must be turning over in his grave when he sees that one of the essential postulates of his philosophic thought is thus mistreated by citizens who are poor, illiterate, but without complexes.

# 6

## VIOLENCE AS ETHIC
## OF EVIL

Pain is what is most intimately self.

—EMIL CIORAN

A man cannot be too careful in the choice of his enemies.

—OSCAR WILDE

It was neither idle curiosity nor a taste for the morbid that had taken me that evening to the police headquarters of the port of Douala. Rather it was the need to reassure myself of my humanity and my capacity for indignation, to see for myself those things that cannot be named, and perhaps to testify about them one day. So it was a kind of citizen's instinct that had led me to wait, with a few other curious people, in front of the big, rusty, iron gate guarded by three drowsy and visibly embittered gendarmes. Someone had phoned me an hour earlier to tell me that the "Coalition" prisoners would be freed at any moment. These five leaders representing a fraction of the emerging opposition had been arrested a few days earlier and no official reason for their custody had been given.

I knew almost all those prisoners: some were established politicians with long careers in the single party before taking the risk of publicly proclaiming their allegiance to a political pluralism in its infancy. Others aspired to becoming leaders of the civil society being reborn and headed associations defending human rights, often hastily created for needs of political positioning. A few weeks earlier, they had set off on a media-covered tour to various Western countries to denounce attacks on human rights by Cameroonian president Paul Biya's regime. While in Paris, they had even made the cover of a magazine, which had captioned the large photo featuring them: "If Biya persists, we'll kick him out!" Such self-confidence hadn't pleased the head of state who, as soon as they were back in the fold, had given firm instructions to the security service to treat them in keeping with their insolence. With no qualms, the Republic's fine torturers had done their work with raise-worthy zeal. Rumors of the ill treatment the prisoners had been subjected to during torture sessions had quickly spread. In this country of everyday violence, it was still difficult for me to remain indifferent to the silent suffering of these prisoners.

## On the "Sovereign National Spanking"

So I'd waited anxiously in front of the entrance to police headquarters. The gate had finally swung into motion with an almost theatrical slowness, with a sinister creaking that would have delighted makers of horror movies. They were a good half-dozen men, coming out of their cells one after the other, under the impassive gaze of their jailers, heads down and their expressions somber. I hadn't recognized them all in the half-dusk, as some had hurried into their families' cars. Samuel Eboua, the oldest of the group, was also the best-known: several times a cabinet minister, he had been the secretary-general of the presidency of the "Republic"—actually, the second most important person of the Republic. On that evening he emerged from the darkness as if walking on a tightrope.

As his family had not been informed of his liberation, no one was waiting for him in front of the sad police headquarters gate. With a hesitant step, he'd come toward me and asked me if I could drive him into the city. It was only when he was getting into my small car with difficulty that I grasped the seriousness of his condition: he could hardly sit down. His bandaged posterior had received two hundred lashes a few days earlier and his injuries had not yet healed. So the insistent rumor circulating in the city was true: the prisoners had been physically tortured.

I was aghast: sixty-seven is certainly not very old. But in this Cameroon where life expectancy was less than fifty years, it was a respectable age all the same, an age at which the body has earned the right no longer to be subjected to chastisement by a police station's torturers. "They hit me! They whipped my buttocks two hundred times!" he said to me with indignant candor, as if to apologize for the time he needed to get into the car. Stunned by this unexpected admission, I was unable to say anything, ashamed of my country and my own powerlessness.

So, like all the other prisoners of the "Coalition," Samuel Eboua had been assaulted, brutally tortured by gendarmes who were simply carrying out orders. Looking at him, I remembered my astonishment on the day when, paging through the phone book, I'd discovered that the National Documentation Center, the main office of the political police and headquarters where opponents of the regime were tortured, had only two telephone numbers: the switchboard and . . . the infirmary.

Samuel Eboua asked me to take him straight to the French consulate in Douala. He was anxious to show the ill treatment of which he'd been the victim to the consul, one of his good friends. He told me about his stay at the police headquarters in great detail, expressing himself with surprise but without anger. He'd been arrested for what he thought would be a routine interrogation. To his surprise, he'd been thrown into a stinking cell with other prisoners, without being asked anything. Then one day, still without really asking them any questions, they'd been stretched out on the ground and strong young gendarmes had given each of them two hundred lashes on their posteriors. It was, they were told, the president of the Republic's answer to their demand for a Sovereign National Conference that was to serve as a Constituent Assembly. In the place of the conference, they were being given a "sovereign national spanking" intended to close all political discussion concerning the soundness and representativeness of the country's political institutions.

He was talking without looking at me, pretending to be more interested in the impoverished lives of the passersby on the street than in our conversation, which I felt was painful for him. To comfort him, I tried to minimize the incident, promising him that quick medical treatment would erase all the scars of this barbarous act. I concealed my indignation by looking at the young girls selling things on the streets who unsettled passersby with their ivory smiles and the ephemeral sight of their breasts.

I drove slowly. The city's streets were full of potholes and the bulbs had disappeared from the street lamps. I was worried about my important passenger's state of health—I shouldn't risk making it worse—and was lost in the dark thoughts assailing me: two hundred whiplashes! How could one do such a thing to a man of his age? Even in a second-rate tropical dictatorship enjoying the favor of the international community, such an act reminiscent of slave holding forts was surprising. Cameroon wasn't fashionable, being neither Zimbabwe, nor Tibet, nor Burma. But all the same, there were limits to indecency. To think that African traditions guarantee a curse and even hell to whoever would raise a hand against an older man! I thought about the torturer who had carried out the "noble instructions of the hierarchy" by making a man who could have been his father or grandfather stretch out on the ground and impassively lashing him with a whip. I imagined the probably hoarse cries that Samuel Eboua must have uttered under the torture and humiliation, and the tranquil detachment of his torturer, who maybe had to drug himself to carry out his task.

## Disguises of Violence

The friend to whose home I rushed later that evening received my indignation with the serenity of a Buddhist sage. He served me a big mug of hot beer and suggested we put things into perspective. Of course, this "sovereign national spanking" suffered by men whose ambition was to overthrow the authoritarian regime was not a great moment of political aesthetics. But the event was not at all surprising: in the tropics anyone who took the risk of defying an illiterate dictatorship knew what was in store for him.

The coldness of such fatalism surprised me. My friend clarified his thinking, reminding me that the brutal treatment accorded these members of the "Coalition" could not be compared to other tragedies that had punctuated the recent political history of Cameroon and Africa. And that was true: in the not-so-distant past, those people would have disappeared without a trace. During several decades of a political independence that was supposed to bring peace and happiness, individuals suspected of belonging to opposition parties were discreetly kidnapped, condemned in extrajudicial trials, and executed. The luckiest found themselves locked away in grim military camps in Tcholliré, Mantung, or Yoko, and came out of them years later, blind or maimed. Although writer Mongo Beti, Cameroon's Solzhenitsyn, devoted works to these tropical gulags, no Western governments were troubled by the situation.

In the 1960s, the army launched napalm attacks against the neighborhoods and villages where militants of the clandestine opposition were hiding. Terror was the only framework for political dialogue. In January 1971, Ernest Ouandié, the president of a banned party, was publicly executed in Bafoussam, after the authorities had noisily exhorted the population to "come out in crowds to attend the event." They weren't really innovating in making death a spectacle: the cult of the morbid, the public spectacle of suffering, and the dramatization of fear were among the favorite weapons of French, British, and German colonists who had ruled this territory as masters for three-quarters of a century.

Even more serious, insisted my friend as he got us more beer: we were neither in Sierra Leone where they cut children's hands off for political reasons, nor in Rwanda where women were raped en masse. That was true too: despite its blunders, the political struggle had not yet become an eruption of violence as sordid as that which had led neighbors and members of the same family to make mincemeat of each other with machetes, to cut off each other's arms or ears. In short, several hundred thousand had not yet been killed; not enough blood had flowed to justify the presence of a few television cameras. "Relax a little," my friend advised. "We haven't even managed yet to get a communiqué from the United Nations . . ." And he went on to explain calmly that the secret to a long life in this country was to understand and accept the fact that everything was an illusion, and above all not to intellectualize the little mysteries of everyday life. Yes, a few apprentice politicians had gotten themselves a whipping. But there was no reason to get all worked up about it. The

fact that they'd been infantilized and their egos brutal-
ized a bit was even rather nice ... "If you start to submit
to the moralism of great virtues, you run the risk of
becoming lucid, which is the beginning of madness."

I came out of that conversation a bit groggy, less due to
the effects of the beer and Douala's nocturnal humidity
than because of the distress into which my friend's nihilism plunged me. What if he was right? What if my stay
in the West and my education at the Sorbonne had soft-
ened my soul to the point of transforming me into an
unconscious romantic? Ought I adapt to the almost
good-natured character of new Cameroonian political
violence and its relatively moderate degree of cruelty?

On another day, I discussed this "sovereign national
spanking" with a compatriot who was a bit less cynical. I
laid out for her the arguments I'd heard in Douala: of
course, it wasn't in good taste to assault good family men
whose only mistake had been to express their opinions.
But their physical integrity was intact and none of them
had been publicly executed. She stiffened with rage: How
could one establish inevitably approximate moral hierarchies among forms of violence that were in her eyes one as
serious as the other? "And all the people they let silently
die of hunger, thirst, or illnesses in hospitals lacking
medications. Isn't that political cruelty and so a form of
violence just as cruel as the others?"

Thus she formulated the problem of the definition of
violence, which depended on each person's subjective
judgment. The beating that the leaders of the Cameroonian opposition were subjected to was obviously a violent

act. But insidious aggression aiming at the psychological integrity of individuals was also a disguised form of violence even more reprehensible. Its modalities were perhaps more sophisticated and its manifestations less spectacular, but its effects could be just as devastating.

## Pornography of Power

That conversation forced me to rethink that famous "sovereign national spanking" and its meaning. I then understood that the government had not been content to have its political adversaries tortured physically and psychologically. It had chosen to proceed in the most brutal manner possible and had wanted this to be known everywhere throughout the country. Several reasons justified this decision: it was first of all the expression of the extreme anger of the president of the Republic and his entourage, shocked by the fact that a group of men with no true political stature had gone abroad to present to international public opinion a far from brilliant picture of the regime. In the dynamics of power relationships between the government and the opposition, it was impermissible to let a precedent be set that would permit adversaries of the regime to gain the psychological upper hand, to gain confidence, and to establish strategic relations with external partners.

Even worse: these opponents had gone to the head office of a Parisian magazine (very influential at that time) and had proclaimed on the front page of this periodical that they would "kick out" of the presidency a head of state who had cultivated the mystique of being God. The Yaoundé regime wanted to inflict an exemplary punishment on men who had defied it without having the means to fulfill their ambitions. The beating they had received when they returned to Cameroon was a way to demonstrate the ridiculous character of their pompous statements to the international press. It also was also a way to intimidate and dissuade all those who harbored the idea of opposing the government. The torture was to wash away the offense to the supreme leader, restore his myth, and reinforce in the collective unconscious the transcendent force of an unshakable power. "When the people no longer fear your power, it is a sign that a greater power is coming," said Lao-tzu.

The government had, for that matter, not bothered with scruples in putting together the usual official gibberish in which it reeled off laws and regulations that the "troublemakers" had supposedly broken. There was no need to give its action a judicial veneer, for discipline was derived from simple brute force, from the "natural" sovereignty of the despot. This is the only norm to which one must conform. The object was to force each individual to resubmit to the authority of the infallible chief and to make them all accept this subjection. The coercion techniques utilized were to restore the disciplinary system by which the speech, behaviors, ambitions, and movements of individuals were controlled, and the will of the all-powerful president accomplished. An exemplary punishment was therefore necessary, even indispensable.

The question before the Yaoundé torturers was that of the choice of punitive techniques. The history of penal procedures and of the systems describing sanctions shows how each of them reveals a way of organizing power. It allows one to distinguish four types of punitive societies: those that exclude the condemned (they are forced into exile); those that organize a form of reparation (justice becoming a sort of payment); those that inscribe a mark (the body of the tortured individual showing the penalty); and those that lock up the persons judged guilty (prison). The punitive mechanisms themselves are less important than their object, and the reason for which each society punishes its "culprits."

The case of Samuel Eboua and his companions was quite revealing as to the functioning of Cameroon's system of "justice." Here, the punishment blended the styles: it involved at the same time confinement, payment in kind (corporal punishment), marked violence, and humiliation as a symbolic form of exile. The government's concern was not to know whether the men in custody had broken some law and committed the misdemeanors or crimes of which they were accused. It was rather a matter of accusing them of having political and social ambitions to which they had no right, and of sanctioning them in a way that would rehabilitate the regime. For that, there was no need of a trial, contradictory debates, or discussions concerning extenuating or aggravating circumstances. Justice merged with punishment to proclaim an infallible psychological truth: the power of the president.

It did not therefore focus on identifiable elements of behavior, but on stated or unacknowledged ambitions. It judged less acts committed or declarations made than intentions. It judged not infractions, but wishes, virtualities of behavior. It attempted to defuse a *dangerousness*. This "justice" was not a proceeding validating the social order, but a system producing an unchanging truth.

All political power is based on the mystery of a gamble: that those governed will accept it, by ignorance or conviction, freely or because they are forced to. Paul Valéry compared political regimes' chances of survival to those of financial institutions, which owe their durability to the fact that it is quite unlikely that all the customers will ever come in on the same day to take out their savings. Cameroon's government was well aware of the political physics of sociopolitical balances and dynamic combinations in an unstable situation. To reduce the probability of a generalized revolt, reinforce its myth, and protect itself from the risks of doubt, it could not tolerate the slightest breach in the collective imaginary. Against the infamous crime of lèse-majesté of which these citizens without real political strength had made themselves guilty, a powerful form of symbolic vengeance was required. The punishment had to be spectacular to strike imaginations and mark minds indelibly. It had to restore the president's reputation and legend of invincibility, revalidate the "social contract" in force, and form the foundation of future memory.

What could better compel the citizens to accept the order of things and adjust their behavior accordingly than a shock treatment for the leaders of the opposition? The punishment had to be corporal and be imposed upon them. It had to constitute a just chastisement for those rebellious bodies who, perhaps without even measuring the seriousness of their acts, had defied the government in its intimacy, at the risk of revealing its nudity. A proportional reprisal was required: even if it meant engaging in a sort of political anatomy and yielding to a sort of pornography of power, the "sovereign national spanking" was considered necessary by the authorities.

## Political Metaphysics of the Spanking

But why choose a spanking and not some other form of corporal punishment that would have inflicted the same degree of pain? To understand this, I had to reexamine the personalities of the men in custody, their relative political weight, and interpret the language of authoritarianism in Africa.

Samuel Eboua, the leader of the group, was also a former minister in President Paul Biya's government and, incidentally, one of his rivals to succeed the previous President Ahmadou Ahidjo. Because of his age and long career in upper-level administrative positions (he held the highest civilian awards), Eboua had found himself at the head of one of the principal opposition parties. He did not, however, have a large personal political following in the country. So for the government, he was a paper tiger. A former apparatchik at odds with the regime, Eboua was furthermore hated by Paul Biya, who felt that he looked down on him. The "sovereign national spanking" seemed like a good opportunity to get even in the most humiliating way possible, without running the risk of having to face a popular uprising.

This was also the case with the other big name of the group. A zealous former activist of the single-party system and an unemployed businessman, he had, a few months earlier, even organized people's marches throughout Cameroon to make fun of the developing opposition's demands for freedom and to reject the introduction of a multiparty system. National television had at the time given him the opportunity to denounce the "birds of ill omen" and intellectuals who dared to criticize Paul Biya and the system of which he was one of the barons. After waiting in vain for the head of state to reward him with some position or other for service rendered, the man had ended up joining the ranks of the opposition—disillusioned. Such an about-face hadn't much pleased the regime in power, which now considered him a traitor.

As for the group's other three members, none of them had a large enough political base to shield them from arrest and torture: one was a lawyer admired for his legal talent and his courage in defending the independent press and human rights activists; another was a resolute, courageous, and imaginative activist who had put forward the idea of a general strike ("Operation Dead Cities") that was later picked up by the opposition parties to paralyze a good part of the country for three months; the last was the self-proclaimed head of a microscopic political party with no know militants, appearing above all to be an exotic agitator. In short, none of the five men had sufficient political capital to protect them from depraved forms of the government's brutality.

From the presidential monarch's point of view, coming up with the spanking was both diabolical and inspired. It was not merely an act of physical torture intended to cause pain. There were also perverse psychopolitical motivations involved. By ordering the violation of the most private and sensual parts of the bodies of his political adversaries, President Paul Biya engaged in a sort of pornography of power whose metaphysics had to be deconstructed. First of all, violating an erogenous zone like the buttocks was a villainous and particularly original way to discredit one's political adversary. The near-public flogging of a man of advanced age like Eboua, a grandfather several times over, reinforced in the collective imaginary the idea that Paul Biya (much younger) was the sole "father of the nation," the undisputed chief, the only depository of authority and truth whom no one could defy without paying the price, even in the most private parts of his anatomy.

This act of torture also served up to the general public the nudity of men suspected of having their eye on the presidency. It deprived them ipso facto of all respectability—the postulate here being that Cameroonians wouldn't want as their political leaders individuals whose incidentally not very sexy posteriors were featured on the front pages of newspapers. The private press, though mostly favoring the Cameroonian opposition, had actually added insult to humiliation: some papers had published on their front page huge photos of the nude or bandaged buttocks of some of the victims of the "sovereign national spanking," accompanied by indignant headlines . . . The torture was thus a double rape: a physical violation of the privacy of the body, since the buttocks contain many nerve endings and are a zone of sexual stimulation; and a political violation and attack on respectability, for the spanking transformed these victims into exhibitionists guilty of indecency—it was symbolically equivalent to publicly exposing their genitals—a sign of political weakness and a serious error of taste. In this country where the aptitude for exercising political power is often expressed in terms of sexual prowess, the chief of state's subliminal message to his adversaries was clear: those who cross him will be publicly raped and will become men who are politically castrated.

Everyone understood very well that the country had now entered a phase of brutal and cynical sexualization of power. Only a few days after this "sovereign national spanking," the leaders of the opposition put an end to the general strike that they had hoped and prayed for, and gave up their demand for a sovereign national conference . . . Suddenly, it seemed preferable to them to respond to the government's injunctions and negotiate minor ministerial positions, rather than run the risk of seeing their private parts flogged and their posteriors spread out on the front pages of newspapers.

## Aestheticization of the Tragic

There is no doubt that the treatment inflicted on the Cameroonian political leaders was humiliating and cruel. I nevertheless had to admit that on the scale of horrors committed by certain men in power in Africa, there had been much worse. In Liberia, for example, the victor of a civil war had turned the slow mutilation of political adversaries into a rarely equaled art of sadism. It was in September 1990. Prince Johnson's rebels had overthrown the military regime of his ex-friend dictator president Samuel Doe. When Doe was attempting to leave the country, he'd been captured in the port of Monrovia, the capital. The man who'd defeated him then had the interminable session of his execution filmed, and distributed video cassettes that are still today selling like hotcakes in video stores of the country's capital.

They show Prince Johnson practically in a trance, seated in the front row, enjoying the spectacle without questioning its ethic and aesthetic, savoring the power of doing what he likes to the body of his prisoner. He sweats, sips at a beer from time to time, belches, and has himself fanned by a woman, like a boxing champion between two rounds. They also show an executioner endowed with a physique befitting his job—his ugliness is almost a caricature. Taking his role seriously, he has the concentration of an astronaut preparing to fly into space. Proving furthermore that he's a serious professional, he meticulously checks the quality of his equipment—whips, daggers, revolvers, and various other utensils.

Prince Johnson shouts orders to Samuel Doe, asking him for the number of his bank account. Realizing after several minutes that his victim isn't in a condition to furnish this information, he gets worked up and orders his soldiers to cut off the former head of state's ears, one after the other. Doe screams in pain, collapses into a pool of his own blood and slowly dies. The camera runs unhurriedly, offering images in black and white whose mediocre quality makes the scene even more unreal. It is difficult not to think of Plato while watching the yield of inhumanity shown by this video, for violence, here underpinned by a triple transgression, is very much in evidence: violation of the physical integrity of the adversary thus dehumanized, as well as of any social pact of nonviolence; perverse sexual arousal of the assassin, who is obviously enjoying the spectacle more than anyone else and is moreover having himself fanned by a woman assumed to be one of his many partners—sadism gives him the opportunity to dominate others and prove his superiority; and profanation of all that might be considered sacred, even in such an environment.

Following these events, Liberia went through a long period of political unrest before electing, for the first time in Africa, a woman as president of the republic. After thirteen years of exile in Nigeria, Prince Johnson returned quietly to the country, where he was democratically elected to the senate. Questioned about any possible remorse he may have regarding his memory of the murder of a political adversary, he said his conscience was clear: "No, God revealed himself to me at the age of seventeen. I applied the law of Moses to Doe: an eye for an eye, a tooth for a tooth . . . And besides, what proves I killed him? Is he dead at the end of the video?" His serenity is reinforced by the philosophical detachment of his compatriots. The French daily *Libération* reported the following comments by a human rights activist in Liberia: "Prince Johnson is a child of the country. Nimba [his county of origin, a few kilometers from the frontier with Guinea] was persecuted under Samuel Doe. Prince Johnson set them free, and that's all. Only intellectuals like you and I wonder about things like that. Look at Charles Taylor [another former president of Liberia, judged for war crimes and crimes against humanity]: he killed more than anyone and he remains the most popular." An aesthete of the art of politics, in sum.

In neighboring Sierra Leone, recourse to corporal punishment had been raised to a comparable level of political sadism. Foday Sankoh, a good family man who was also the leader of the Revolutionary United Front, made it a point of honor to inscribe the mark of his power onto the bodies of his victims. Being satisfied with murdering them would have been too dull and ordinary. His soldiers drew lots for civilians (men, women, and children of all ages) whom they met on their path and dismembered them with machetes. Here too, nothing really new under the sun: the Greek historian Herodotus reports that, several centuries before the Christian era, Scythian soldiers scalped their adversaries and used their scalps as towels. But Foday Sankoh wanted to outdo the Greeks. To him, war was above all a battle of rituals and symbols, and dismembering victims an elevated form of aesthetic refinement. He took more pride in the four thousand or so one-armed citizens with which he'd populated his country than in the 150,000 deaths caused by his rebel movement.

An even more Machiavellian form of the aestheticization of political violence is the resort to rape. Human rights organizations justly stress the indelible character of this form of violence—notably when children are its victims. Sexual torture is now part of the panoply of psychological means used in all conflicts in Africa. Rape is thus supposed to inflict on the enemy not only an insurmountable psychological defeat, but also to "soil," "debase," and supremely humiliate the category of the population that is the most precious because it is responsible for the reproduction of the species. The rapes of Bosnian, Croatian, and Serbian women during the civil war of 1992–1995 popularized this way of "decorating" the tragedy of war. Woman's precious body, considered an ethical sanctuary and preeminent aesthetic reference point in all societies, thus becomes the place where sexual fantasies of drunken soldiers are satisfied, the locus where the absolute power and domination of the conquerors is expressed. They take a morbid pleasure in depreciating the intimacy of their adversaries' wives. They believe that they are winning the psychological war once and for all by dishonoring what the enemy values more than anything else. This was the case in Rwanda during the genocide of 1994. It is still the case in the Democratic Republic of Congo where various armed factions have been fighting since 1997 for control of the country's mineral resources. A perverse conception of aesthetics through which they project their subjective vision of the sensory and the beautiful: in their eyes, war is won not only in combat between men on the battlefield, but also in the expression of sexual domination and the satisfaction of basic desires.

## The Strength of the Weak:
## An Ethic of Evil

Let us return for a moment to Prince Johnson, Liberia's ear cutter. His explanation of his acts of cruelty is not very sophisticated. One can easily imagine him with a faint mischievous smile when he said he'd simply applied the will of God, who supposedly revealed Himself to him when he was seventeen years old. But he's not identifying with Bernadette Soubirous, the virgin of Lourdes to whom Saint Mary appeared during her adolescence. He offers this mystic explanation of his conduct with the naïve expectation that it would be stylish to situate his actions on a cosmic plane. He does not, however, wish to be considered a simple visionary. For he'd scarcely put forward the revelation argument when he found another, in his opinion more practical and powerful: "And besides, what proves I killed him?" he asked ingenuously. "Is he dead at the end of the video?" In other words, what proof is there that he's really a murderer? After all, can this crime be directly attributed to him if the video, the principal piece of evidence, shows soldiers other than him perpetrating the most horrible acts? He, Prince Johnson, was only the man behind the violence; the ultimate responsibility for the murder would lie with those who held the weapon.

Cheap sophistry? No matter. His arguments are part of the nihilist principles of violence often heard from those who consider the notions of guilt and innocence arbitrary, or at least two sides of a single coin. Existence being for them a mad dash toward nothingness, it seems silly to them to try to assign responsibilities in the Darwinian struggles imposed by survival.

Foday Sankoh, the Sierra Leonean arm chopper, had said the same thing when he was arrested. Astonished at seeing himself charged, he modestly pointed out that the original manifesto of his rebel movement was entitled *Footpaths to Democracy* and that its slogan was: "No more slave, no more master. Power and wealth to the people." And, in any case, his combatants and he had no choice: if they hadn't terrorized the populations and neutralized their political adversaries, suffering and death would have been inflicted on them.

Johnson and Sankoh do not even define themselves as heroes, for in their context any act of bravery is childish. The poverty and reign of the arbitrary that regulate daily life testify above all to the fact that existence is a form of aimless agitation, to which those who choose not to commit suicide are forced to submit—at their own risk. So one shouldn't delude oneself: all action takes place against a background of emptiness and unreality. The human being is basically a body doomed to ruin. The fact of being able to use it as they wish to temporarily satisfy a few fantasies of power does not change a thing in the fundamental equation of daily life. And a few outbursts of indignation, short-lived, by the way, by self-proclaimed human rights activists in the West will not change this state of affairs.

For these two monsters, excessive use of physical force to establish a relationship of brutality and inhumanity with others is a distinctive feature of man; life on earth is inevitably a struggle against oneself and against others, and violence is the mandatory weapon the weak need in order to exist. Recourse to physical torture and murder are protective mechanisms necessary to the functioning of society. Violence is essential as a means of restoring balance to conflicting forces, indeed as a way of giving an ethical dimension to the evil that constitutes the fabric and background noise of existence.

This tragic reading of history by two illiterate warlords of the West African bush combines two views of violence: that of Plato who saw violent people as tyrannical beings taking sadistic and cruel pleasure in dominating others in order to prove to themselves their own superiority; and that of Sigmund Freud, who understood violence as a weakness of human nature, the symptom of a neurosis. Of course, reducing violence to a natural form of behavior amounts to excluding all human responsibility for it, and thus justifies in advance all the crimes of those who resort to it. But this is exactly the reasoning of many African warlords. From their point of view, the assertion of someone like René Girard that man becomes human not because he gives in to his drives by using violence, but on the contrary because he refuses violence and invents other mechanisms of social interaction is so sweetly naïve that it makes them smile.

## Mandela's Moral Dilemma

How can one free oneself from violence in a world where it serves as sustenance for people who believe in nothing and expect nothing from life? How can one free oneself from the dictatorship of evil when everyone comes to terms with it? And why, for that matter, objectively choose to differentiate oneself from it when the collective imaginary seems to have made of it an ordinary thing, a constant of daily life? In his memoirs, Nelson Mandela implicitly admits that he wasn't asking himself these questions when he decided to convince his activist friends of the African National Congress (ANC, a nationalist movement) to create an armed branch of the movement. Living underground under the apartheid regime, the South African leader had seen the cruel asymmetry in the power relationship between the nonviolent methods of his organization and the solemnly proclaimed brutality of a government that had engraved racism into the country's constitution. He had seen with sickening discouragement the massacres of children, women, and black workers who dared to ask peacefully for a minimal amount of humanity. Faced with the exponential number of victims of state violence, and the devastating effects of apartheid on the souls of his compatriots, Mandela concluded that the nonviolent philosophy advocated by the ANC since its creation in 1912 amounted to guilty naïveté. The arrogance with which the South African authorities treated the most reasonable demands had convinced him of one thing: faced with a psychopathic regime, one had to adjust the ethic of one's methods of combat.

"Sebatana ha se bokwe ka diatla! (The attacks of the wild beast cannot be averted with only bare hands!)" he proclaimed regularly in the Xhosa language during clandestine meetings of his organization's leadership, to stress the ineffectiveness of nonviolent combat in such circumstances. And he went on to explain that violence was already a fact, and that it would be better to channel it toward the noble aims of the ANC than to continue to adopt a semipassive position whose result was the daily deaths of many innocent people. To which some of his colleagues answered: "Nonviolence has not failed us. We have failed nonviolence." Mandela managed to persuade his friends to abandon the sacrosanct principle that had been at the heart of their political strategy for half a century. He was even put in charge of creating and heading an armed branch of the organization. "I who had never been a soldier, who had never fought in battle, who had never fired a gun at an enemy, had been given the task of starting an army," he writes. "It would be a daunting task for a veteran general much less a military novice."[1] Calmly he set about creating an armed group called Umkhonto we Sizwe (Spear of the Nation), training experts in the use of dynamite and choosing military targets. Who would have thought that the man who now embodies peace and tolerance, the conscience of suffering humanity, the advocate of reconciliation with all enemies, the aesthete of politics, was also the theoretician of an ethic of violence?

Mandela did not choose this path without hesitation. After all, he was walking in the steps of Mahatma Gandhi, whose nonviolent philosophy had been formed after traumas experienced during his stay in South Africa. The decision to opt for violent action was not only an admission of failure, of the inability to convince and transform the other, of the impossibility to achieve what Martin Luther King called the double victory—vanquish one's own demons and those of the adversary. It was also a serious setback for his conscience, a true moral defeat. For he had to face up to two contradictions: either continue to reject violence in the name of the pacifist theory of nonresistance to evil and refuse to tarnish its ethical demand; or resort to violence to try to put an end to violence, so as not to let his people die. In the end, he concluded that the second contradiction was better than the first, and that it was necessary to resort to dynamite explosions in order to vanquish apartheid. Just as the fact of taking up arms against the Nazis was "a sacred, absolute, indisputable duty."[2]

After the famous "sovereign national spanking" in Cameroon, a few people also raised their voices to denounce the "hypocritical naïveté" of those who thus took refuge behind a false ethical demand and proposed contenting themselves with nonviolent forms of resistance. It would be better to reject passive acceptance of the brutality of a state that had become mad. I remember one evening reading graffiti on a wall in the working-class neighborhood of New Bell (Douala): "Andze Tsoungui [the minister of the interior] is going to die tomorrow at six o'clock." Justification: it was necessary to resort to limited violence to put an end to great violence. The murder of a tyrant seemed to them an eminently ethical act, a source of moral capital gain for society. This philosophical choice was supported by the idea that even nonviolent forms of resistance, incidentally ineffective, hid an intrinsic violence that devalued their moral authority. Vladimir Jankélévitch would undoubtedly have approved of such an approach, as he justified the moral dilemma posed by recourse to violence: "There's no use telling us that we're contradicting our own principles; we are not contradicting them; we are doing the best we can in a world where Tolstoy's utopia, which is to convince the enemy through the force of love and forgiveness, is a bleating of silly sheep."[3]

The same sort of moralization of violence can be found in the promoters of armed guerilla bands whose bloody action punctuates the history of the African continent. The rebel soldiers who, coming from Rwanda and Uganda, had overthrown the regime of Zaire's dictator Mobutu Sese Seko to reestablish the Democratic Republic of Congo, followed the same line of reasoning: armed violence seemed to be the way to economize on human lives. The leaders of the Rwandan Patriotic Army who had overthrown the fascist regime responsible for the genocide of the Tutsi in 1994 also explained that their violence was necessary, indispensable, and ethical. Now it so happens that those who had perpetrated this genocide were themselves the hostages of an older rancor, which they justified by the suffering of the Hutu people during the period of semislavery imposed on them by a feudal regime dominated by Tutsis and supported by the Belgian colonizers ... Here we find ourselves *bound to violence* (to use the title of Malian author Yambo Ouologuem's novel)—that is, truly in the very heart of psychological determinism.

In this type of reasoning, it is certainly advisable to avoid the moral amalgam between the action of the guilty and that of the victims, an equivalence that results in dissolving responsibilities and trivializing evil. But it is striking to see that both parties, in turn, claim the other is responsible for the situation; accuse one another of diabolical actions; and unrelentingly persist in wanting to give an ethical dimension to violence and evil. Each camp explains its least glorious acts by past events, lack of justice buried in the country's political history, and moral debts and claims held by one side in relation to the other. Studying the sources of information on the Rwandan genocide, philosopher Fabien Eboussi Boulaga is struck by "their heterogeneity, the doubtful value of some of them, too apologetic, muddled by remorse, a guilty conscience, self-justification, and finally the predominance of the official, conformist speech of the victors and their allies."[4] He notes, however, that despite everything there is a factual core, a truth of each situation that, even if it is "haunted and tormented by the impenitent or equivocal silence of the protagonists of both camps, will always resist the reductions and negations or the perverse inversions of bad faith." Even then, one must be able to accede to it, and approach it with the necessary critical distance and serenity to identify it and use it in the best way possible.

African historical experience shows that the modes of justifying violence founded on the historical legitimacy of rancor or even the desire to exercise justice often come up against the sad truth of practice: they quickly lose their moral glow and dissolve into the evil they claim to repair. The armed rebels who had triumphantly entered the streets of Kinshasa to chase from them the remnants of Mobutu Sese Seko's despotic regime rapidly turned into cannibals of power, becoming themselves the target of a counterrebellion that was morally as ambitious as it was feeble. Just like the hotheaded Black Panther activists who had traded the naïve nobility and generosity of their ideals of emancipating African Americans for the establishment of an armed revolutionary socialism ended up offering J. Edgar Hoover, the Machiavellian head of the Federal Bureau of Investigation, a politico-moral foundation to validate his policy of assassinating activists said to be incorruptible. Simone Weil was right when she said: "Force is not a machine for automatically creating justice. It is a blind mechanism which produces indiscriminately and impartially just or unjust results."[5]

## Nihilism and Private Violence

The other night in Washington, at a concert by the young African American singer Wayna, I heard her introduce one of her songs by pointing out that she lives in Prince George County, Maryland, which, according to official statistics, is both the place in the United States where the black community has the greatest purchasing power and where each year there are the greatest number of incidents of domestic violence. This contradiction gave her the idea for a song in which she imagines all those pretty black women living in the county's fine homes, driving around every day in big luxurious cars, and in the evening hiding behind the immaculate walls of their fabulous villas to receive physical punishment from their husbands.

Intriguing. Even so, the validity of the statistical inferences of this statement that inspired a melancholy song needs to be checked. For people of various ethnic groups and social categories—including a large number of fairly poor African American citizens—live in Prince George County. In order to confirm or refute Wayna's impressionistic commentary, a microsurvey would have to be conducted to identify the social classes and the precise locations from which distress calls of battered women originate. Furthermore, it is possible that the rate of domestic violence in other American neighborhoods, cities, and counties is quite a bit higher than in Prince George, but that, for various reasons, the victims don't contact the police. It's hard to imagine that the sadly famous poor sectors of large American cities (Washington, Chicago, Los Angeles, the Bronx in New York), rife with organized crime and other illegal activities, have less domestic violence than a county in Maryland.

But what does it matter? Let us suppose that Wayna's statistics are trustworthy: that would mean that there is no correlation between African American citizens' purchasing power and their marital behavior. So then one would have to wonder about the origins of this "private" violence that governs relationships between members of the same family and within black communities.

It is worth noting first of all that there is nothing specifically African about the phenomenon: women live perilously in Mexico City as well as in Turin, Kabul, or Djakarta. Family law, which in some societies gives a legal framework to various forms of private violence against women, children, or people belonging to castes considered inferior, is part of this situation. In all societies, the social contract has always been founded on coercion. It therefore assumes the acceptance of a minimal amount of violence—like public violence that, with or without individual consent, is carried out in the name of all. The rules of social coexistence and the norms that are unwritten but validated by collective memory are then put forward to justify it.

Release mechanisms of private violence in the black world often have the distinctive feature of reflecting and magnifying the sociohistorical perspective in which the relationships between the social groups take place. Daily life is then too often dominated by the memory of oppression. It becomes obvious that the denial of humanity inflicted on the black man during several centuries of slavery and colonization weighed more heavily than one thought. The internalization of self-hatred is still expressed in lack of self-esteem, self-flagellation, and the permanent doubt about oneself and the humanity of those whom one resembles—notably women. Across generations and despite education, the memory of this suffering continues to infect the souls of millions of men throughout the African continent. Its principal manifestation is the perversion of power relationships within the family, between the sexes and the generations, and the constant desire to perpetuate the humiliation and oppression of which one has never truly ceased being the victim.[6]

Philosopher Cornel West ascribes the high rate of violence in the African American community, particularly within couples, to the persistence of the idea of a harmful "white supremacy" accepted and perpetuated today by yesterday's victims. He stresses the "self-niggerization" of black peoples, which too often leads them to despise and denigrate themselves, and inflict violence on one another. This can be seen in the use of the word "nigger" in public discourse, which gives rise to a lively debate among African American leaders. The late poet Maya Angelou and actor Bill Cosby have seen in it a lack of self-respect and a poison that seeps into minds and facilitates violence among blacks. As for West, he thinks one shouldn't attach too much importance to words. First of all because the use of "nigga" (a more intimate pronunciation than "nigger") by African Americans to address each other is actually a mode of identification and fraternization, an affectionate term of complicity, indeed an expression of endearment. Then, because one must go beyond simple symbolism, actions taken seem to him to be more essential than the language used. "I know African-Americans who never utter the word nigger but who all the same suffer from a serious lack of self-esteem." The proof? Martin Luther King or Malcolm X could have used this taboo word as many times as they wanted without anyone being shocked or doubting their commitment to the fight against the oppression of the men and women of the black community.

Private violence cannot be explained solely by historical factors. It is also connected to the fact that it is not easy to serenely follow moral precepts in times of material shortage. Material poverty quickly becomes collective bitterness. Faced with skepticism, the great codes of ethics then lose their charm. Those who suffer the most from this fall into a sort of state of inebriation that for them legitimizes recourse to violence.

So we return to Wayna's question, which is pertinent: Why does not emancipation from material poverty free man of his bellicose instincts? Perhaps because those who succeed socially still feel as threatened by failure as those who are at the bottom of the ladder. They don't believe in the solidity of the reasons for their success, which they know are often precarious. Success thus appears to them as a trial and a suffering all the greater because the risk of a fall back into destitution is constant. Obsessed by fear and doubt, they conduct themselves in the same way as those who continue to languish in indigence. Whether aimed at people like themselves within the community or at their conjugal partners, violence is the expression of this feeling of helplessness. It is a way of proclaiming their authority and warding off impecuniousness. Like a soft drug that puts them into a state of unconsciousness and unreality, it also enables them to endure the passing days. A subtle form of nihilism, it is then a flight from this vision of their own degradation. Here too, it is meant as an ethic of evil.

# CONCLUSION

## NIHILISM TO TAME DEATH

Who am I? I don't even know the hour of my death.

—JORGE LUIS BORGES

Repent one day before your death. This very day.

—HEBREW PROVERB

The news of my father's death plunged me into a feeling of helpless distress from which I've never really recovered, despite the passing years. Not simply because of the tragic circumstances surrounding this wrenching event, but also because of the painful lessons of existence that it would inflict upon me in the course of the following days, months, and years. Time has passed, but the wound has remained intact, open, and silent.

It was one of those sad, beautiful blue-skied days that exist only in Douala. One of those characteristic September Douala days, with faltering light, a grimacing sky, stifling humidity, and a funereal sun. A strange phone call from my cousin Léo had transpierced my nerves and hurled me into a mental universe that I hadn't known existed. The habitually jovial and teasing tone in which he always spoke to me had given way to curt speech: "Papa Robert had an automobile accident. They took him to the hospital." Léo, who usually expressed himself very clearly, seemed to be stammering on the phone, unable to give me any more information on what had really happened, nor on where my father was. He'd simply asked me to wait in my office while he tried to learn more.

He then came to get me and drove me around for a long time, giving evasive answers to my questions about where the accident had taken place, how serious it was, and the name of the hospital my father had been taken to. He took me to Papa Emma's, his older brother, who was also my father's best friend. Not knowing that Léo had until then kept from me the most painful information, Papa Emma greeted me with his blunt directness:

> "Papa Robert has left us. Just like that. In an automobile accident."
>
> "I thought he'd had an accident . . ."
>
> "Didn't Léo tell you he died instantly? I'm sorry. You're a man now. You have to take the family in hand. We'll make the funeral arrangements."

I have no clear memory of the moments following this exchange, nor the places I went to afterward. My mind had gotten bogged down in all manner of feelings, from astonishment to the most violent rage. My father was barely sixty years old and was making plans for the next sixty. In addition to the affection we'd felt for each other, we had managed to create a space of complicity that was my most precious possession. Precisely at the moment when I was beginning my career as a young executive for the preparation of which he'd sacrificed all his savings and devoted his love, at the precise instant when I was hoping I could tell him and prove to him that his sacred calling had not been in vain, fate was separating us in the most violent manner.

I remember thinking about the equally painful death of my mother quite a few years earlier, in the prime of her life—she who had brought me into the world at the age of sixteen. There too, injustice had aimed well, breaking my semiadolescent heart to hurl me without preparation into the irascible world of frustrations and responsibilities. Listening to Papa Emma's recommendations with difficulty, I tried to restrain my rancor against the arbitrariness of existence and keep the emotionless expression and proud bearing that my father would probably have expected of me in difficult circumstances. There, where he was, my father was certainly watching me with his concerned smile, wondering whether I would pass the test of decency—that test by which he took the measure of a man.

## Tectonics of Emotions

The adrenaline of the shock and the imperious necessity to prove myself equal to the tragedy helped me get almost unscathed through the bureaucratic and family formalities linked to the management of his death: the torture of going to the morgue of Yaoundé Central Hospital, which seemed to have been deliberately constructed like an antechamber to hell; the torment of administrative formalities in the Kafkaesque offices of the Ministry of Finance where my father had worked; and the ordeal of family get-togethers where those present tried to outdo each other in noisily demonstrating their incandescent compassion, and where every obscure cousin and most distant aunt imposed their views on the decisions to be made, each one speaking more loudly than the other.

There was also the stoicism of my friend and guardian angel Richard, constantly reminding me of the first words of Epictetus's *Manual:* "Of things some are in our power, and others are not." What was not in my power was the tragic event of the death and the behavior of others. What was in my power was the way I perceived it, my judgment, and my actions.

Not many of us, however, attempted to preserve a modicum of good behavior and decency in the circumstances. In general, the announcement of the death was met with hysterical cries, mournful howls, and even apoplectic fits. In some of these reactions, anxiety regarding death was much stronger than the feeling of injustice at knowing that my father was now gone. I was able to say with a certain degree of assurance that Mami Marie, my favorite aunt and the sister my father was closest to, felt like I did the raw wound of the wrench, the brutal, invisible violence of the cry that is not uttered, that heart-rending cry that burns one's throat and annihilates speech. On the other hand, it seemed to me that I could detect in the crocodile tears of an uncle or cousin very different things: either their manufactured emotions were part of a general tectonics suitable to the occasion (it was appropriate to display one's sadness in an exaggerated way); or they expressed justifiable vexation, due above all to the fact that this generous man to whom they had all constantly turned for solutions to their financial or family problems would now no longer be here; or finally they expressed anxiety before something unnamable and incomprehensible, fear of death as an undecipherable metaphysical experience, for which we have no empirical reference or credible system of representation.

The viewing was the most painful moment, the one whose images I have since then tried subconsciously to purge from my memory. I'd had to confront my father's decaying face in the morgue of the Yaoundé hospital to believe it. The horizon had suddenly come toward me, enclosing me in the narrow square of this dark, dusty room where my father was now stretched out on an iron bed rusty with age. I'd remained immobile, troubled by the certainty that this image of a stiff silhouette that had become unrecognizable and these stifling odors bathed in my sisters' tears and moans would forever be part of my life. A sudden wave of fright from very far away, from my childhood perhaps, had shaken me violently: perhaps the feeling of undergoing the disintegration of my own body or seeing the dissolution of my own consciousness, and the certainty of watching, powerless, my own drowning?

Before that particular moment, the sad news had not yet seeped into me totally. Like Jacques Madaule, I was still telling myself: "I know that I will die, but I don't believe it." Because it is nearly impossible to live without the primordial illusion of the refusal of death. Death was for me a final deadline that was both artificial and mythical, constantly put off. It was a matter concerning people I didn't know, or else neighbors and distant members of the extended family. In the smoky half light of a Cameroonian morgue, it suddenly took on the appearance of a menacing, unmanageable reality. It became an implacable experience that took away not only my father, but also the amount of metaphysical hope I needed to continue to live innocently.

At that moment I began to realize that something serious was happening. All the conversations I thought of having with my father and that I'd constantly put off suddenly came to mind, sharpening the feeling of guilt that I'd had for a long time. An infinite number of memories and plans flooded to the surface of my memory, appearing suddenly as impossible dreams. I then experienced "the incredible indiscretion of death" of which Emil Cioran speaks when he tells of the closing of the coffin of one of his friends: "Atrocious weather, setting so ugly that it makes death and thus life more insignificant and more laughable than they are. That metro passing close by, that horrible bridge across the way, those factory chimneys, then these coffins laid out in the hall, and the bustling activity of the workmen nailing down covers with detachment . . . That's where one must go to be cured of all the torments that come from taking things to heart. No sorrow or worry will survive such a spectacle."[1]

No. Coming out of there, I had not gotten over my existential worries—quite to the contrary. Condolences and encouragement came from all sides, including from phantoms I'd lost sight of ages ago. A colleague known for his bad taste trundled out the argument used by Plutarch to calm his wife at the death of their daughter: "Why weep? You were not afflicted when you did not yet have a child; now that you no longer have one, you're in the same situation." Besides the fact that I'd had a father all my life, the essence of such a witticism intended to comfort did not take into account the strength, the legitimacy of the affection, and the intimacy with the deceased person—not to mention love, this "swearword" that Plutarch apparently didn't know.

The intention of those surrounding me was to try to ease my grief. My grandmother Mami Madé, queen mother of the Banas, told me, for instance, that my father had simply left for an immanent beyond from where, according to our customs, our ancestors constantly spoke to us. So, in the final analysis, it was simply a matter of a long journey that we would all be called upon to make one day. One of my sisters who was very pious commented that God called to his side only those whose help he needed to continue to care for us from that other world at once distant and close to ours. The *eternal absence* of our father that we dreaded was in fact a new form of presence. Thanks to language, death thus ceased being a dangerous, gaping opening into nothingness, to appear as a sort of window into the *other* life.

I heard the old sages repeating all around me that death is an integral part of life on earth and that we ought to accept it. These remarks did not keep me from wondering: So why all this weeping? Why all these old women rolling on the ground in vexation? Why didn't they come to terms with it as they would with the absence of someone who had simply set out on a long journey? You have to get things into perspective, one of my uncles explained to me: first, the fact of weeping together helped lighten the grief of the wrench that I myself felt intensely; it was also an age-old ritual showing affection, the symbolism of a good-bye, a way of marking the traumatic aspect of the departure of a man who was leaving the world of the living. Tears were a punctuation of finality.

The idea of passively accepting death because it is merely a phase of existence raised the problem of dealing with uncertainty. For each of us, life and death are the certain components of a closed circle in which uncertainty concerning the date permits hope. It offers us the leeway we need in order to act, to express our moods and our nihilistic outbursts, to prepare and polish the legacy or the image that we leave to posterity. Life is therefore indeed saturated with the perfume of death, but in a way that gives each citizen the possibility of making his own way, of giving a meaning—even if provisional—to his earthly journey. Those who think of their death constantly may perhaps succeed in honing the priorities of their existence, but that does not help them die. So it is more profitable not to worry excessively about it.

And yet, the more they tried to comfort me, the more I realized how much my father was part of myself, of my own person. His abrupt departure suddenly made me feel his body as an extension of myself. The heavy family and social responsibilities he took on made his Herculean life more legitimate than mine. The death of this indispensable man suddenly became for me the essential philosophical experience: in a certain way, it signified my death, for it erased the subconscious biological barrier between me and nothingness. It made the death of others less impersonal.

I suddenly realized that the notion of life expectancy had meaning: beyond a certain threshold, there were only a limited number of years left to live—inevitably. This mental calculation expressed my consciousness of a man pondering his becoming. This is a difference between us and animals: we can live a life from which we can at the same time detach ourselves to observe it from an external perspective. At the source of my grief, there was thus not only the pain of the emptiness left by my father's departure, but also a shock between these two realities: the certainty of living while being programmed to leave this world, and the possibility of seeing things from a different perspective in order to speculate at leisure about one's becoming, without the limitation of time applied to life. Death, to me, was no longer a social abstraction, but a first-person trauma—it was the beginning of my own death. This irrevocable moment has never left me.

## Social Grammar of the Funereal

Making the funeral arrangements led to some friction. No one had the bad taste to suggest burying my father in a cemetery. First of all, those places where corpses are collectively packed in do not really exist in the customs of western Cameroon. And then, due to his lineage and the aura of notability he had in the village, my father's ultimate resting place had to be chosen in close collaboration with his cousin, the king of the Banas. Consensus was reached that "tradition" should be honored and he be buried with dignity behind the family house that he himself had built not far from the royal palace.

With my grandmother Mami Madé and the king, we discussed the practical details of the burial and funeral. We first meticulously studied the traditional lunar calendar and its week of eight days, each one corresponding with the day on which secret societies met and special customary ceremonies were held. The appropriate dates fell into place. The king then gave me the list of formalities to perform and of things I had to buy: a white chicken to be sacrificed during a ritual; two or three goats to give to key individuals in the village who had played an important role in my father's upbringing; whiskey for this notable or that grandmother (even in the hills of western Cameroon, Scotch liquors were so appreciated that they were now part of "tradition") . . .

All the members of the family had initially seemed to agree with these decisions, even managing to make me think that their common priority was to do things efficiently and with dignity. In actual fact, some of them did not want to argue over the place of burial or the date of the funeral, but waited to unleash their egoisms and passions on the details of organizing the event, the funeral rituals, and ceremonies. As soon as I returned to Douala, my house was invaded by members of the extended family—cousins, uncles, aunts, neighbors—and a few individuals with questionable motives who all claimed they'd had a close relationship with my father. That entitled them to kindly give me orders, to dictate to me details of the funeral arrangements. Displaying amazing creativity, they firmly gave me a long list of formalities to fulfill in order to give my father a burial worthy of the name. The list included not only usual expenses like paying the morgue for preserving the body or buying a coffin and funeral wreaths worthy of the deceased's social standing, but also putting together a publicity campaign in newspapers and on the radio to inform the general public of the imminence of a great event.

They also asked me to budget enough money to organize big feasts for hundreds of guests of honor scattered across the country, pay their hotel bills (since there weren't enough suitable lodgings in the village to put them up), and have clothing especially made for the funeral. The scarcely concealed agenda was to take advantage of the tragic event that was bringing us together in order to polish the family's prestige and reposition all its members on the social and political scene. There was also an admirable form of nihilism in this attitude: a spectacular funeral was an elegant way to thumb one's nose at death, a refusal to succumb to fear, a way of "frivolizing" tragedy.

Just one problem: all those good souls were obviously counting on me, a young bank manager, to finance their brilliant, extravagant ideas. My interlocutors were out of luck: I was in no mood to let myself be impressed by people taking advantage of a posthumous closeness to my father to try to convince me to finance their fantasies of grandeur. Besides, I'd been close enough to my father during his lifetime to remember very precisely his feelings about each one of them. So, not bothering with polite phrases, I gave them my opinion in no uncertain terms and pointed out to them that, as eldest son, I would organize the burial and the funeral in my own way—as discreetly as possible.

Amazement! How could I dare oppose decisions made by people older than me? Had I completely lost my head? What legitimacy did I pride myself on, I who wasn't even thirty years old and was neither married nor head of a family? . . . The news that I wasn't quite myself spread as quickly as a Bantu secret—faster than the speed of light. One of my aunts, one of the country's most famous female jurists, immediately mobilized a family crisis committee to attempt to bring me to my senses. "You stayed in Paris too long!" they told me. "You don't know a thing about our traditions anymore! There's nothing Bamiléké about you anymore! The White Man's school [i.e., education] has driven you mad! . . . You want to violate customs and prohibitions. You've become much too Western and you're running the risk of angering the ancestors . . ." In the

threatening statements they were making about me, the words that constantly came up were "taboo," "curse," "sacrilege," "treason," and so forth. We were enmeshed in mythology. And I continued to answer calmly: "I may be mad, but I like this madness and I have no desire to resemble you." They stared wide-eyed and spit out swearwords with eyes raised to the heavens.

My friend Richard had to play mediator between my aunts and me to avoid a family scandal that would probably have made headlines. This engineer-turned-businessman appealed to the economist in me, recommending that I approve the family requests, absurd as they might be. He told me, in substance, that I should think of them as a social symbolic system of redistribution of wealth, since the funeral was an opportunity to show generosity and to feed the greatest possible number of people in the village who, because of their state of material poverty, didn't have complete meals every day. He also recommended that I accept my uncles', aunts' and cousins' requests on the simple basis of a cost-benefit analysis of the problem: by satisfying their requests—including the most harebrained ones—I was in a sense purchasing my tranquility and giving myself a priceless internal peace.

Richard then summarized for me the basic philosophy of the Bamiléké cosmogony in one sentence: "Death is their reason for living." Because all human bodies had the same fate, regardless of social class and the places where they were buried, and because everyone came into this world in the same way and left it for this same earth that received their remains, death cast a light on the

fundamental philosophical choice offered to man: live in the love of one's family, knowing that the temporality of such an existence is what gives it savor and meaning; live in peace with others so as to leave with a light heart when death looms; or else live outside oneself and outside others, live without an emotional connection with the community, detached from social contingencies, so as to die as one has lived, without making the slightest wave, since one would then have lived in a sort of perpetual death. Faced with such an alternative, my uncles and aunts had made a nihilistic choice: that of seeing life as a bright parenthesis whose end should be celebrated like fireworks, like the handwriting of eternity. Hence the social activity characterizing the organization of grandiose funerals, and the serene decision to go into debt and poverty if necessary in order to color an existence that had refused to be ordinary. This sort of plea convinced me to submit to the family demands. Without deluding myself, however.

## A Ludic Funeral

The burial was sad but dignified. There was a Catholic priest and a pastor, but above all notables of the secret societies that manage the village and to which my father took pride in belonging. Christian prayers alternated with pagan songs. Not from a proclaimed wish to be ecumenical, but simply because no one had even considered the necessity of conciliating different things. This philosophical cohabitation of contraries was so natural that no one could have thought this way of doing things in-

congruous. In a sort of unexpressed nihilism, death was both conceivable and livable. At that precise moment, it was indeed only a phase of existence.

In their prayers and homilies, the priest and pastor encouraged the family, sketching a linear interpretation of the painful event we had just experienced. They presented the death of my father as a new phase of his life, a new birth, a logical future. As a result, the present moment we were living that evening was a sort of interstice between the past and the future. They exhorted us to make the best use of it so that each of us would merit, when our time came, the journey to paradise. As to the old notables who spoke in the name of the pagan secret societies of the village, they calmly expressed the opposite point of view: in their opinion, there was no established hierarchy between life and death, and no linear process linked the two events. For these two states coexisted in each of us: because human nature is in essence multiple, and there is no dichotomy between body and soul, each person was at the same time dead and alive. Since the funeral aimed not at rehabilitating the memory of the deceased father—there was no need for that—but at trivializing the very idea of death, they thus managed to slay the tragedy shown by our tears and grief. And to invalidate the simplistic symmetry of revealed religions: death should not be lived as a birth in reverse, no more than the future could be a new life the right way around. Birth, life, and death were simply three aspects of a single reality, simultaneously visible.

The solemnity of the burial was matched by the celebratory fragrance of the funeral a few hours later. My grandmother had asked me to bring her very small amounts of palm oil, salt, and food that she used for a sober ritual to accompany my late father to the world of the spirits. The women of the village each had large bowls of food, as well as palm wine and other local beverages. All my friends from Douala and Yaoundé had come, they too bringing cases of beer, red wine, and even champagne. Hundreds of people thus filed onto the family property, offering their condolences, sharing a drink, and engaging in friendly discussions about anything and everything.

This great conversation took place against a permanent background of traditional music played outdoors by frenzied instrumentalists. Balafons—African xylophones—little talking drums, and various wind instruments were used to produce boisterous rhythms and create an atmosphere that at times bordered on extravagance and would certainly have pleased the stoical hedonist that my father had been. Before the sublimity of this music that seemed to address my innermost thoughts as well as the beyond, I remembered Cioran's claim that the organ gives to death a status that it does not naturally have. Here, it was rather death that gave style to the music.

This almost ludic funeral reached its apotheosis late in the night, when almost all the inhabitants of the village had piled into the large courtyard to proclaim my father's name, sing in unison, dance with every fiber of their being, and drink alcohol with the fervor one would put into fighting an enemy. Around me, people of all ages sang and danced feverishly. Wambé Chuêwa, my grandfather's successor and, as such, the patriarch of the family, was himself in the heart of the action. Nothing in his getup or behavior suggested that he was an authentic mathematician with a graduate degree from the Sorbonne. Dressed in a large tunic of woven beads, he was wearing a spectacular headdress decorated with parrot feathers and pounding with ever renewed vigor on a drum that didn't really need coaxing to send out its lugubrious tones. Next to him, uncles and cousins who also looked as if they were in another world played the tom-tom and balafon.

All the members of the family were asked to dance in a circle, all in step in the middle of the courtyard. I thus found myself next to my aunt, the famous jurist, the very woman who had expressed such shock at my initial refusal to finance ceremonies that I considered a waste of money. She too was dancing furiously, her sharp eyes strafing me regularly to check how much enthusiasm I myself was putting into this exercise. Then, coming close to me, she whispered into my ear in French, with her Parisian accent: "You, who turned your nose up at us, have you realized now how important this ceremony is for the whole village?" Then, pointing at the patriarch Wambe Chuêwa: "Look at him. He has a doctorate in mathematics from the Sorbonne. And yet he's the one playing the sacred drum! And you, you think you're ahead of us. You scorn our traditions when you haven't yet even gotten as far as defending a doctoral dissertation!" My eyes had turned toward the patriarch: my aunt was right, for he was in seventh heaven. He seemed very far from there, perhaps in the stratosphere. He seemed to be looking straight ahead without seeing anything, pounding the sacred drum like a visionary. I wondered what his former comrades with whom he'd studied topological structures or differential geometry would have thought of such a scene.

In this collective exorcism of death as a sad inevitability, the old people were the spryest and the most enterprising. With sometimes half-closed eyes, they clapped their hands in cadence and shouted with their hoarse, almost cracking voices. Those bodies that I thought were worn out gave no sign of vital fatigue. This impromptu explosion of what looked like joy was yet another form of nihilism. While elsewhere old age is endured as expressing "the irreversibility of becoming that is the fundamental pathos of existence" (Vladimir Jankélévitch), that evening in the village I saw something else in my grandparents' detachment: a haughty scorn for the wear and tear of life and the unavoidability of the end, a refusal to conform or submit to the biological rhythms imposed by average longevity. Dance was not only the means of ridding bodies of pain and cleansing minds of sadness. It was about transforming vital rhythms. It also reflected a conception of time aimed at lengthening human life. It helped reinvent natural entropy, which has always been man's vocation, and reshape the economy of our existences. For time stretching away necessarily changes styles of life and relational postulates: an old man who dances with conviction rejuvenates all those around him who are less young, which modifies the dynamics of feelings. In the final analysis, my father's funeral revealed the possibility of longer slices of life—in short, of a metaphysical rejuvenation. Watching the crowd, I thought of Balzac: "Death is too certain; let us forget it."

The singing and dancing stopped momentarily only when my cousin the king of the Banas spoke to say simply that my father had had "an intense life, full and useful to the entire community," that he had played his part on the scene of our collective existence. For this reason, the king categorically forbade anyone to "mourn his death." He insisted that we accept serenely the idea that it was a departure for this other journey with the ancestors to which we, the living, did not yet have the right: "The essential paradox is that one must accept the idea of dying to have the right to live. This tacit contract that we all have with death is the condition of our existence." I then understood that death was a metaphysical dialectic that imposes itself on us. By putting an end to life as I knew it, death made it possible. Death was both its final obstacle and its indispensable developer.

So the angst felt when faced with death was erased by the collective need for lucidity. We were no longer in the usual fundamental illusion, this "essential cheating" of which Jankélévitch spoke, that consists in believing that death applies to others, to neighbors, to passersby on the street, but not to oneself. The beyond appeared as an invisible world adjacent to the visible world, serene and just as legitimate as that of our daily existence. Death should be accepted as an object of unconcern, an ordinary phase of our earthly journey. Each person ought, moreover, to minimize it by living life to the fullest. Armed with such a nihilistic view of death, I saw in my father's departure, when all was said and done, "a stroll in the firmament of destiny" (Jankélévitch).

Still today, many years later, I continue to think about it. I sometimes wonder if his keen consciousness of life ended with his death—the disappearance of his body. On some days of intense memory when I think I hear his voice again, his mocking laugh and his lessons of life, I'm inclined to think that his spirit has obviously survived the decomposition of his body and that, from where he is, he's watching me with his disillusioned air. Has his death incited me to better prepare mine? Did it awaken me to the laughable, ephemeral character of my own life, as the old village sages said in their nihilistic flights of oratory during the funeral? I'm not so sure. The seismic violence of his death, the authenticity of the tears of his sister Mami Marie, and the depth of the emptiness created by his eternal absence have certainly forced me to revise the priorities of my existence. And yet, the more I think about it, the more it seems to me that I have simply learned to subdue my own suffering. Time has passed but sorrow is still with me. Grief has coagulated somewhat in my body while remaining intense in my mind. Perhaps, for that matter, it is grief that gives meaning to my steps.

# NOTES

# ACKNOWLEDGMENTS

# INDEX

# NOTES

## Introduction

1. The black world, an inevitably controversial geographical and historical categorization, includes not only the populations of sub-Saharan Africa, but also those of diaspora, imposed or undergone, since the time of the slave trade. It is thus not surprising that discourses on present-day Africa often intersect with those formulated, for instance, in the United States concerning African Americans. See, for example, Cornel West's analysis, *Race Matters* (Boston: Beacon Press, 1993).

2. See Tommie Shelby, *We Who Are Dark: The Philosophical Foundations of Black Solidarity* (Cambridge, MA: Harvard University Press, 2005).

3. *Voices of the Harlem Renaissance,* referencing New York's famous black neighborhood, is the subtitle of the anthology *The New Negro* (New York: Touchstone, 1925). Edited by Alain Locke, it brings together texts by black intellectuals and artists who wanted to give the world a sampling of the cultural effervescence and freeing of the American black imaginary.

4. Jean-Paul Sartre, *Black Orpheus,* trans. S. W. Allen (Paris: Présence africaine, 1963), 18.

5. Achille Mbembe, "Afropolitanism," trans. Laurent Chauvel, in *Africa Remix: Contemporary Art of a Continent,* ed. Simon Jnami (Johannesburg: Jacana Media, 2007), 26–30.

6. Kwame A. Appiah, *In My Father's House: Africa in the Philosophy of Culture* (New York: Oxford University Press, 1992); Valentin Y. Mudimbe, *The Invention of Africa: Gnosis, Philosophy, and the Order of Knowledge* (Bloomington: Indiana University Press, 1988).

7. Octavio Paz, *The Labyrinth of Solitude,* trans. Lysander Kemp (New York: Grove Press, 1961, 1985), 9.

8. This and the quotations above in this paragraph are from the epigraph to Paz's *Labyrinth of Solitude.*

9. Ibid., 10.

10. Paul Bourget, *Essais de Psychologie contemporaine* (Paris: Plon, 1937), xix.

11. Emil Cioran, *Cahiers, 1957–1972* (Paris: Gallimard, 1997), 132.

12. Michel Foucault, "My Body, This Paper, This Fire," trans. Geoff Bennington, in *Aesthetics, Method, and Epistemology,* vol. 2, ed. James D. Faubion (New York: New Press, 1998), 416.

## I. Desire's Ruses

1. John Keats to Fanny Brawne, September 13, 1819, in *Letters of John Keats to Fanny Brawne* (New York: George Broughton and Barclay Dunham, 1901), 36.

2. Burkina Faso means "the land of worthy men of integrity."

3. Jorge Luis Borges, *Conférences* (Paris: Gallimard, 1985), 120.

4. In her *Natural History of Love* (New York: Random House, 1994), Diane Ackerman states that love is an intangible concept whose importance, necessity and marvels are recognized by everyone, but whose significance is never agreed upon: "We use the word *love* in such a sloppy way that it can mean almost nothing or absolutely everything" (xviii). Proving her own theory, incidentally, her book offers no definition of love.

5. Jorge Luis Borges, *Ultimes dialogues avec O. Ferrari* (Paris: Ed. Zoé, 1988), 78.

6. Jean-Claude Kaufmann, *Sociologie du couple* (Paris: PUF, 1993), 5.

7. Édouard Glissant, *Le discours antillais* (Paris: Seuil, 1981), 97.

8. bell hooks and Cornel West, *Breaking Bread: Insurgent Black Intellectual Life* (Boston: South End Press, 1991), 12–13.

9. Léopold Sédar Senghor, "Black Woman," in *West African Verse: An Anthology*, ed. Donatus Ibe Nwoga (London: Longmans, 1967), 96–97.

10. Gloria Chuku, "Women in the Economy of the Igboland, 1900 to 1970: A Survey," *African Economic History* 23 (1995): 39.

11. A French cartoonist and comic strip writer. He was killed on January 7, 2015, in a terrorist attack on *Charlie Hebdo*, along with other staff.

## 2. I Eat Therefore I Am

1. Emil Cioran, *Entretiens* (Paris: Gallimard, 1995), 28.

2. Claude Lévi-Strauss, *Du miel aux cendres* (Paris: Plon, 1967), 276.

3. Paul Veyne, "The Roman Empire," in *A History of Private Life*, vol. 1, ed. Philippe Ariès and Georges Duby (Cambridge, MA: Harvard University Press, 1987), 188–189.

4. Michel Foucault, "What Is Enlightenment?," in *The Foucault Reader*, ed. Paul Rabinow (New York: Pantheon Books, 1984), 41.

## 3. Poetics of Movement

1. John Martin claims that the dancer's movements create kinetic stimuli to which the audience generally responds by invisible muscular mimicry; see *The Dance in Theory* (Princeton, NJ: Princeton Book Company, 1965).

2. Emil Cioran, *Cahiers, 1957–1972* (Paris: Gallimard, 1997), 650.

3. Pierre Souvtchinsky (1892–1985) was a Ukrainian artistic patron and writer on music. A friend of Sergei Prokofiev and

Igor Stravinsky, he was the real author of the book *Poétique musicale* (1942; translated in 1947 as *Poetics of Music*), published as by Stravinsky.

4. All one has to do is listen to his compositions on albums by Mike Stern (*These Times* [2004] and *Who Let the Cats Out?* [2006]) to be convinced of this. The artificial character of the distinction between "vocal" and "instrumental" is quite obvious: each medium interferes with the other and makes its mark on the work of creation.

## 4. The Savor of Sin

1. See Célestin Monga, *Un Bantou à Washington* (Paris: PUF, 2007).
2. Emil Cioran, *Cahiers, 1957–1972* (Paris: Gallimard), 645, 917.
3. Cf. Emily Oster, "Witchcraft, Weather and Economic Growth in Renaissance Europe," *Journal of Economic Perspectives* 18, no. 1 (Winter 2004): 215–228.

## 5. Ethic of the Uses of the Body

1. This vision is set out in his *Discourse on the Method*. But Descartes seems less categorical on the question of the body in his *Passions of the Soul,* published a dozen years later.
2. Georges Balandier, *Conjugaisons* (Paris: Fayard, 1997), 219–220.
3. Achille Mbembe, *La naissance du maquis dans le Sud-Cameroun* (Paris: Karthala, 1996), 16.
4. Catherine Ndiaye, *Gens de sable* (Paris: POL, 1984), 31.
5. Ibid., 30.
6. See Daniel S. Hamermesh, Xin Meng, and Junsen Zhang, "Dress for Success: Does Primping Pay?," *Labour Economics* 9 (October 2002) 361–373; and Daniel S. Hamermesh, *Changing Looks and Changing "Discrimination": The Beauty of Economists* (Austin: University of Texas, 2005).
7. *Hodgdon v. Mt. Mansfield Company,* Vermont Supreme Court, November 6, 1992.

8.  Jean-François Mattéi, opening address to the First International Meeting on "Le corps et son image" [The body and its image], Paris, September 20, 2002.

## 6. Violence as Ethic of Evil

1.  Nelson Mandela, *Long Walk to Freedom* (Boston: Little, Brown, 1994), 239.
2.  Ibid.
3.  Vladimir Jankélévitch, *Penser la mort?* (Paris: Liana Levi, 1994), 125–126.
4.  F. Eboussi Boulaga, introduction to *Le génocide rwandais: Les interrogations des intellectuels africains,* by F. Eboussi Boulaga and Alain Didier Olinga (Yaoundé: Éditions CLE, 2006).
5.  Simone Weil, *The Need for Roots,* trans. Arthur Wills (New York: G. P. Putnam's Sons, 1952), 243.
6.  This phenomenon of latency is comparable to the mystery that economists encounter when they study, for instance, the causes of unemployment. They observe that very often a problem persists quite a long time after the factors that caused it have disappeared. This negative memory is called "hysteresis."

## Conclusion

1.  Emil Cioran, *Cahiers, 1957–1972* (Paris: Gallimard, 1997), 560.

# ACKNOWLEDGMENTS

A strange thing sometimes happens to economists: they are taken seriously. Such was the case when Roland Jaccard, a well-known Swiss scholar and publisher at the Presses Universitaires de France, telephoned me a few years ago at my World Bank office in Washington to invite me to write a trilogy of travelogues in the form of sociology and philosophy books. Jaccard, who had reviewed two decades earlier for the French daily *Le Monde* my short diary from a trip on the shores of the Red Sea, wondered how an economist and a banker by profession could be a nihilist at heart. He was puzzled at the apparent disconnect between my professional life as an international civil servant working in a large development institution to fight global poverty, and my philosophical stance as an admirer of Emile Cioran, Friedrich Nietzsche, and Fabien Eboussi Boulaga.

That was the genesis of the French version of this book, *Nihilisme et négritude* (PUF 2009), and a couple of others. I am grateful to Jaccard for having given me the opportunity to think and write about Africa not as a "foreign," exotic, black or white entity but as an integral part of a subtle and complex world. I am also thankful to friends, colleagues, and mentors who have encouraged me in this rewarding intellectual journey.

I cannot list them all but should mention Kwame Anthony Appiah, Olivier Blanchard, François Bourguignon, Julia Cagé, Mamadou Diawara, Hippolyte Fofack, Cilas Kemedjio, Ambroise Kom, Justin Yifu Lin, Alain Mabanckou, Achille Mbembe, Edouard Akame Mfoumou, Valentin Mudimbe, Gérémie Sawadogo, Joseph Stiglitz, and Jean-Claude Tchatchouang.

As a reader of André Gide, I long wondered whether his famous quote "Families, I hate you!" was actually inspired by his understanding of the dynamics and mysteries of life in African families. Thanks to the unconditional love and support of some of my own family members, I have learned to put things into perspective. My literary work and my life have been enriched beyond explanation by the care and support of several family members, including Florence Djache, Simon Inou, Alain Georges Juimo, Ferdinand Edimo Nana, Xavier Sajo Nana, Yasmine Ndassa, Richard Nouni, and Anne-Mireille Tchiencheu.

Last but not least, this English version of the book could not have been released without the enthusiastic support of Ian Malcolm, my editor at Harvard University Press, and the hard work and patience of my translator, Madeleine Velguth. I would like to take this opportunity to also acknowledge my intellectual debt to other translators of this book, most notably Estela de Abreu (Portuguese) and Anshan Li (Chinese).

# INDEX